HOW TO
PRAY
WHEN YOU'RE
PISSED AT
GOD

IAN PUNNETT

HOW TO
PRAY
WHEN YOU'RE
PISSED AT
GOD

OR ANYONE ELSE FOR THAT MATTER

HARMONY
BOOKS · NEW YORK

Copyright © 2013 by Ian Case Punnett

Published in the United States by Image, an imprint of the Crown
Publishing Group, a division of Random House, Inc., New York.

www.crownpublishing.com

IMAGE is a registered trademark, and the "I" colophon is a
trademark of Random House, Inc.

Library of Congress Cataloging-in-Publication Data
Punnett, Ian, 1960–
    How to pray when you're pissed at God / Ian Punnett.
        pages cm
    1. Anger—Religious aspects—Christianity. 2. Prayer—
Christianity. I. Title.
BV4627.A5P86 2013
242'.4—dc23   2012036546

ISBN 978-0-307-98603-0
eISBN 978-0-307-98604-7

Printed in the United States of America

Jacket design by Nupoor Gordon

10 9 8 7 6 5 4 3 2 1

First Edition

CONTENTS

Contents

AUTHOR'S NOTE

Ever been pissed at God?

Sound like blasphemy? Many might agree with you, but did you know that there are literally dozens of angry prayers to God in the Bible? Some prayers express anger at God, and others demand that God settle a human grievance with some Divine justice—but have you ever even heard them in your house of worship? Chances are, rarely.

On the cross, Jesus quoted from one of those angry prayers when he felt abandoned by God. He wasn't the first. Moses, during moments of anger and frustration, boldly stood up to God, as did all-around biblical good guy Job, and even David, the Goliath-killing, Bathsheba-bedding leader of God's chosen people. Though the circumstances of each confrontation were different, each of those holy men ended up improving his relationship with the Divine in the process.

Is the very thought of expressing anger to God making you uncomfortable?

That's okay, I get it. Sometimes we don't like to admit we're angry to those around us, those fleshy people we call friends, neighbors, strangers, and family, not to mention spouting off to God, who is invisible most of the time.

Maybe we're afraid that if we say what we're feeling we'll go to hell or a house will fall on top of us. Maybe we don't even know we're mad as hell with God, so we internalize our feelings and in turn yell at someone who cuts us off on the freeway or is rude to us in a shopping mall. Or maybe instead of giving it to God, we give it to someone we love. Ouch.

But there's good news! When times are tough, when you feel like you're getting the short end of the stick, when you're mad as hell and can't take it anymore, it's okay to be pissed, and it's even okay to be pissed at God. In fact, for your spiritual health (and in turn your physical and mental health) it's important to let God know just how upset you are about anything that's going on in your life. Maybe you've been cheated on, maybe you or a loved one is going through an illness, maybe you've lost your job or suffered a major career disappointment, maybe you cannot get comfortable with issues around your sexuality, maybe you have depression, maybe you cannot get over painful memories from your family of origin, maybe your kids are growing up and don't want to spend time with you, maybe you're just so overcome by all the violence and mayhem that seems to affect our world every day and you just can't understand it anymore—this book is for you.

Before we go any further, though, let me tell you a little bit about why I love this subject and why I have dedicated years of my life to trying to understand the emotion of anger and our relationship with God.

As a weekend host for almost fifteen years on *Coast to Coast AM,* the wildly popular syndicated overnight radio show, I have shared a microphone with broadcasting legends such as Art Bell and George Noory. During the week, I have been a major market talk show host, a Top 40 deejay, and the morning man on a couple of hard-rock radio stations. Yet, while it might surprise some radio listeners, I have been interested in faith matters my entire life, and I financed my tuition for a Master of Divinity from Columbia Theological Seminary by playing the rock hits on 103 WKDF in Nashville and 96rock in Atlanta and doing talk radio. I even did a couple rotations interning as a hospital chaplain and gave years of service as an ordained deacon in the Episcopal Church funded by myTalk 107.1 in the Twin Cities.

Should it seem odd to you that the person you were listening to playing heavy-metal cuts or talking about the Kardashians, government conspiracies, or Bigfoot on the radio was an active member of a faith community, imagine how shocking it was to those who knew me only as a preacher on Sunday morning to realize they had been listening to me the night before noodling around on the radio.

Yet during all those years on the air, I was always amazed at how much faith came into play, especially when listeners would call in to comment about a particular news story, get angry with a guest, ask a question, or just get something off their chest. That being said, I have never led a double life. I carry my faith and my desire to understand the mysteries of life with me everywhere I go and it plays a part in whatever I do. Listeners must have picked up on this because they have never been shy about reaching out. I'd like to think I'm approachable. Like anybody, I struggle and succeed in equal spurts. Mine is a tattered faith.

Now, I understand that for some people, faith in the Divine is like a beautiful white suit they keep in a cedar-lined closet to be taken out only on Sundays and special occasions. Their faith-suit is dazzling to the eye, stain-free, and it looks very much like it did the first day they tried it on. That's just not me. I wear my faith like an old corduroy jacket that has patches on the elbows and scars all over it from my haphazard mending. It's no less precious than anybody else's, I believe, but I often use my faith as a blanket when I'm lounging under a tree on a lazy afternoon or balled up as a pillow to sleep on at night. My faith-jacket has coffee stains, is hopelessly wrinkled, and never looks right at dinner parties anymore. Even so, after all these years it keeps me warm and protected.

I have a wrinkled, frayed, corduroy kind of ministry too. I wear my clerical collar only when I am supposed to—it literally chafes my neck—and I try not to wear my religion on my sleeve. For example, I never sport a visible cross because if I can't convince you that I am a Christian by the way I behave, then the jewelry is pointless anyway.

Still, I've been quite fortunate over the years to have

people come to me with their problems, and while I listened to callers on the radio and sat at times with a mother or father or child in need, I was always perplexed when someone had a tough time articulating his or her anger about a certain situation or anger toward God.

❧◯◯❧

As of this writing, I am the deacon of an old, cool, drafty, supposedly haunted Gothic church in the Midwest that can be a little creepy at night. I maintain a regular preaching schedule for a variety of denominations and wear all sorts of fancy-schmancy vestments that can sometimes look pretty corny. I pray every day but I should pray more. My mind wanders during hymns I don't understand. I love my faith, but sometimes when I think of all the regulations of organized religion I have to wonder: Would Jesus insist on all these rules?

Most of my rules are purely internal. Here are some of mine.

Ministry is not about me. Prayer time is precious. Don't waste God's time. Our time on earth is precious. Don't waste the time of those with whom you worship. Get to the point. When you get to the point, try to make it a good one.

Back when I was in divinity school, a professor of homiletics (the study of kick-ass preaching) once threw out this challenge: "When you finish writing your sermons," she said, "ask yourself this question: Did Jesus die in agony so that I could say this?"

Pleasant thought, right? But I have to tell you every time I preach—just like every time I pray—I want to believe that what I had to say was worth God's time. To me, when it comes to God-talk, if you aren't saying *something*, you aren't saying *anything*.

I also believe that God wants nothing less than honest prayers. There is a place for lighting candles and blowing holy smoke, but sometimes things happen in our lives—we are betrayed by a friend or a loved one dies unexpectedly (or expectedly—both losses are hard)—and the best way to process these problems is through prayer. Prayer can yield answers.

Of course, if there are understandable reasons that bad things have happened to us, it's easier to get our minds around what it all means (or at least might mean). But when seemingly no one is to blame, when we are experiencing tragedy through no fault of our own, when everybody is telling us that God is trying to send us a message—but that message truly, absolutely, totally sucks—why shouldn't we call to heaven and say, "Hey, what the hell?"

Yes, challenging God can be downright scary, but based on the number of biblical heroes who confronted God with their angry feelings and in turn flourished, wouldn't that suggest that God expects a little pushback sometimes?

In the chapters ahead I will make it clear that we are not taking our faith seriously if we think that God needs us to leave candy and flowers on heaven's doorstep every morning. God is big enough to take our anger, and the God I love never favors those who spend their day kissing God's holy and ineffable . . .

But I digress. Our spiritual lives often resemble our sex lives: Everybody goes through a dry spell now and then. When we feel anger (or any emotion for that matter) and we try to repress it, things begin to build up and can result in sadness, anxiety, weight gain, insomnia, and a number of other ailments that require many rolls of paper towels. Living a healthy life means taking care of ourselves—mind, body, and soul. As I will show you, by not taking spiritual care seriously, we may be taking months off our physical lives. Praying truthfully, really digging deep down and expressing ourselves, is the whole point of prayer in the first place. When we can do this we will experience peace. We will be transformed.

So, in those moments of frustration, anger, and despair, when you put your head down and your hands up but nothing comes out, it's good to know how to pray when you're pissed at God—or anybody else for that matter—in a productive and respectful manner. How do we do this? One way—and the way of this book—is to recover the ancient art of angry prayer, which simply means bringing our honest emotions about life and about God *to* God.

How to Pray When You're Pissed at God is not "the last word" on angry prayer, but it might be the first words you have ever heard on the topic. By the end of the book, it is my hope that you'll understand the role of anger in our lives, the benefit of honest prayer, and the need for honest, angry prayer in the lives of the faithful and faithless. My approach will be equal parts scientific, psychological, theological, and just plain old Midwestern commonsense. You will see that when we are angry, our neural processes and subsequently our whole bodies perform badly with dire physical, mental, and spiritual consequences. And really, who needs that?

When you first start out, try not to be self-conscious about how angry prayers come out of you. We're all just kids here playing in God's giant sandbox. The more you learn about angry prayer, the more you will see that there is a simple formula that has been used for thousands of years that will bring you closer to others and closer to God.

❧◯◯❧

A few more words before we begin. It should be noted that this is not a book about identifying the role of God in the midst of tragedies like Japan's tsunami, the aftermath of Hurricane Katrina, or the world-changing day of 9/11. Understanding how a just, all-caring God can exist in the face of evil and pain . . . well, no one's figured that out yet to the satisfaction of everybody, and probably no one ever will. This is life. This is what we have to deal with, and none of us should be wasting time bemoaning the reality around us. If we don't like something, then we should stop bitching about it and do something productive about it. While never losing sight of the Golden Rule, "Do unto others as you would have them do unto you," we can be the change we need by remembering the Bronze Rule: "The Lord helps those who help themselves." Sometimes when we put our shoulders into the boulders that are obstructing our progress we find out that we were falsely accusing God of wanting us to suffer in the first place, but don't mistake me; this is not an attempt to "defend God" when it comes to pain and suffering. This will become clearer as we move along.

In fact, I am not concerned with defending God at all. My brain is too puny to read the mind of God, so I will not concern myself with God's relationship with humans. Instead I will be discussing only our human relationships with each other, our relationships with ourselves, and our relationships with God. Sometimes before people of faith can get on their knees, they have to get some things off their chest. This book will help you do that.

So how do we process anger when it pertains to the Divine? First we need to understand what anger is and how we can tell when we're experiencing it. Next, the importance of prayer in general has to be understood both as a function of our spiritual and mental health and as a contributing factor to our physical health. Putting those two ideas together, you'll see that angry prayer is a key but underutilized positive force in our lives.

I understand that you will have questions:

> Do angry prayers really work?
>
> Will God be offended if we pray through our anger?
>
> Don't we have to watch our words when we pray?
>
> Is there a biblical structure to an angry prayer that I can follow in writing my own?
>
> How do I get started?

The answers to the last five questions are:

> Yes.
>
> No.
>
> You'll be surprised.
>
> It's been in your Bibles all along.
>
> Turn the page.

Chapter One

IS IT OKAY TO BE MAD AT GOD?

*On a Sunday in November 2010, Buffalo Bills wide re-*ceiver Steve Johnson was so angry after having bobbled what would have been a winning touchdown against the rival Pittsburgh Steelers that he tweeted this to his many thousands of followers: "I praise you 24/7!!! And this is how you do me!!! You expect me to learn from this!! How?? I'll never forget this!! Ever!! Thx tho!"

No word on whether God actually follows Steve Johnson on Twitter, but apparently a lot of God's followers do.

After his digital outburst, Johnson received a barrage of criticism not only from Bills fans but also from sports talk show hosts and callers from around the country. One guy who posts comments online under the name "A Bit Concerned" reflected the backlash when he wrote, "Steve should start attending Sunday school or Bible study more often to get better acquainted with GOD. Or perhaps even a hearty chat with the Bills' chaplain will help him cope better. More importantly it is time to grow up and own his mistakes." Receiving little support,

Johnson retreated days later and responded to the criticism with a new tweet: "No, I did not blame God, people. Seriously?"

Too bad. Steve Johnson should not have backed down. Before he buckled under the pressure from those too nervous or too timid to express anger and frustration toward God, Johnson was in the company of angels.

The Bible is full of heroes who took their relationship with God seriously enough to honor their Creator with honesty. In fact, anger between the Creator and creation is older than the Bible itself. For example, years before the Bible was even written down, Moses and God quarreled after the children of Israel got drunk and bowed down to a graven image of another god. After all God had done to free the Israelites from bondage in Egypt, his people wanted to replace him with a golden calf. God was as angry as someone who has just come home from a hard day at work and catches their spouse cheating in the marital bed. God declared to Moses that this was the last straw, and that, as God, God was going start again with humanity. A lesser prophet might have stepped aside and let the Creator wipe out creation, but Moses had the chutzpah to challenge God on whether or not God's reaction was fair. God backed down.

Now, you might be saying, Moses's cause seems more righteous than a dropped football pass—and you'd be right (unless you're a Buffalo Bills fan). But the lesson is the same: God can handle the occasional angry outburst. God can handle being questioned.

The biblical story of a righteous man named Job is another example of somebody who stands up to God and lives to tell about it. In the not-so-surprisingly titled book of Job, God and Satan treat our protagonist like a lab rat. Why? To determine whether a prosperous, faithful man would curse God if everything he loves is taken away. So, long Bible story short, God allows Satan to wipe out Job's fortune, kill Job's seven sons and three daughters, and then cover his body in boils. Job feels that God was unjustified in making a good man suffer, and he tells God exactly how he feels—despite tremendous pressure from his friends to keep his mouth shut. Job's wife, on the other hand, has another thought. She suggests he "curse God and die." Job does neither. Instead of cursing God, he calls God out on the series of tragedies he has suffered and he demands answers.

Let the battle begin! Job jabs with "Why?" God counters that "God is God," and God could crush Job's head like a grape if God felt like it—an argument Job has a hard time refuting. Yet after a few rounds Job wins the match (arguably) because he is not punished for questioning God as his friends had feared he would be. In a surprise ending, instead God sides with Job and rebukes Job's friends for being such candy asses (I'm paraphrasing here). Subsequently, Job's suffering is turned into a blessing—he ends up with even more stuff than he had before, including seven new sons and three new daughters (the Bible even makes the rather tacky point that the new living daughters are better looking than the old dead ones—yikes). Job lives another 140 years boil-free. The Bible doesn't concern itself with how Mrs. Job feels about God. Just sayin'.

So what's the moral here? Well, there are many, but one is that God wants us to speak our truth when we are experiencing disappointment, resentment, and anger and that it's perfectly fine to express our beliefs in times of crisis. In the end we have to get good with what God has planned for us, but we do not have to go quietly. Quick side note: The theme of "I will not go quietly" is powerfully represented in the movie *The Apostle*, written by, directed by, produced by, and starring Robert Duvall. In a pivotal scene, a charismatic, slightly psychotic Pentecostal preacher argues so loudly in prayer with God that he wakes the neighborhood. The preacher's mother, played by June Carter Cash, answers a complaining call from an angry neighbor by saying, "That's my son, that is. I'll tell ya, ever since he was an itty-bitty boy, sometimes he talks to the Lord and sometimes he yells at the Lord. Tonight, he just happens to be yellin' at him."

Even Jesus of Nazareth—hands-down the most obedient son who ever lived ("Wait, you want me to find twelve friends who are willing to die, perform lots of miracles, pick a fight with the local officials, and then get myself nailed to a tree? Sure, Dad.")—does not go quietly either. Crucified, bloodied, and thirsty he cries out in agony quoting the first line from Psalm 22: "My God, my God, why have you forsaken me?" It is one of the saddest, most desperate prayers in a Bible full of pain, frustration, and anger.

In fact, prayers of the pissed off are everywhere in the Bible, so this is probably a good time to talk specifically about the Book of Psalms, a collection of 150 Hebrew songs and prayers that are some of the best-loved spiritual writings of all time and a source of inspiration for billions of members of different faiths around the world. Commonly the psalms are broken up into five or six main "themes," including but not limited to psalms of praise, psalms of thanksgiving, royal psalms, psalms for special occasions, so-called "curse psalms," and psalms of lament.

Most of these categories are self-explanatory, but two need more illumination because they interconnect. Let's look briefly at the curse psalms and the psalms of lament.

Curse psalms are dominated by expressions of anger and frustration, and are characterized by grievances directed at others and at God, sentiments that can get really ugly. The general consensus among scholars is that Psalms 5, 6, 11, 12, 35, 37, 40, 52, 54, 56, 58, 69, 79, 83, 109, 137, 139, and 143 are grouped together as curse psalms, while other psalms have curse elements to them. Lament, on the other hand, is a tricky word in relation to these prayers because *lament* means "an expression of sorrow or grief." The problem, then, is that there is a difference between saying, "I am sad, God," and saying, "God, this really sucks that I am so sad, and you really could be doing something about it, God, but you're not." Lament psalms are often laced with anger toward and resentment of God. For example, Psalm 5 doesn't just lament God's seeming unwillingness to strike out against the enemies of the person who is praying; it tactfully (more or less) schools God on how God should be dealing with what the writer perceives as bad people:

> *For there is no truth in their mouths;*
> *their hearts are destruction;*
> *their throats are open graves;*
> *they flatter with their tongues.*
> *Make them bear their guilt, O God;*
> *let them fall by their own counsels;*
> *because of their many transgressions cast them out,*
> *for they have rebelled against you.*

Suffice it to say there are many such prayers for the pissed off in the Bible, demonstrating that there is a long history of praying in anger to God and at God. There's also a long history of skittish theologians trying to contextualize those angry prayers in order to "take the curse off them." Case in point, Dr. Ralph F. Wilson, director of Joyful Heart Renewal Ministries and author of *Experiencing the Psalms,* argues in his writing that the angriest psalms are an example of "pre-Christian attitudes" and are "not to be examples of our lives as Christians." Not surprisingly, I disagree and find that attitude intellectually dishonest and unproductive. First of all, if we follow Wilson's Christian logic, anything in the Old Testament could reflect a "pre-Christian attitude," so all the psalms, the writings of the prophets, and even the Ten Commandments could be ignored. But doesn't common sense dictate that we should expect psalms that reflect anger toward God if anger is a natural emotion experienced by everyone from young children to sports heroes to saints?

Dr. Julie Exline, professor of clinical psychology at Case Western Reserve University in Cleveland, Ohio, explained another aspect of the debate about angry prayer in an e-mail: "A national survey included an item on anger toward God back in 1988 and revealed that about two thirds of Americans admitted that they were sometimes angry at God." But Exline's recent research into "God focused anger" indicates that "there is some reason to believe that these estimates are on the low side. For example, people who see anger toward God as morally wrong say that they would be less comfortable admitting these feelings to others (including researchers)."

Even in the comfort of prosperity, some people find it

difficult to maintain a relationship with the Divine. In maddening times, as in the events of war, natural disasters, famine, and family crisis, faith can be so problematic that prayers can be a lot less "Holy Bible" and a lot more "Holy $h#!"

If you have ever found yourself so angry at God that you have lost the ability to pray, you may have been standing on the threshold of a new level of faith (although it might have felt more like a breakdown than a breakthrough at the time). Oftentimes in our human relationships, the tighter the relationship, the tighter the tension, and it's no different with God.

I can speak from experience. My breakdown/breakthrough came at the tail end of my high school graduation and continued through my first year of college. During that period an older man from my church who had been like a father to me was fighting for his life in a hospital. Because my real father lacked the emotional resources necessary to be a fully dimensional dad, this neighbor had been a very important and beneficial influence in my life as I was growing up. He was my role model. And this great man was now on the verge of death at such a relatively young age? He was married, could be such a great father—how could God do that? In a just universe, why would God do that?

I was angry so I prayed. I begged God to allow me to switch places with him. If there were a magical cliff from which I could have thrown myself, and my death would have meant that he could have been restored, I would have jumped without hesitation. But as things got worse for him and my prayers became more desperate, I began to lose my faith that there was any point to trying to be righteous at all.

The breaking point came when in the depth of my anger I became what is called a "protest atheist." It's not that I stopped believing in God; rather I had stopped believing in a God who was worthy of being worshipped. Every day I simply did what I wanted regardless of whether it was consistent with my family's values. I stopped paying any real attention to my studies. I even lost my virginity to a registered nurse I barely knew on the hood of her Corvette under a full moon just to make sure God would notice.

And yet, from appearances anyway, my life kept getting better. To paraphrase from the book of Job, I cursed God but I did not die. I was offered jobs, raises, parts in college performances for which I didn't even have to audition. I had stopped going to church, I had stopped reading the Bible, and I had stopped praying, but nothing bad happened. In my religious worldview leading up to college, this kind of cause and effect would not have made sense at all.

At some point I realized that I still yearned for my relationship with God. While there was a slim hope for this man who had been like a father to me, though, there didn't seem to be any hope for me and the Lord. As it turned out, my mentor indeed did survive, albeit with lasting damage to his body. For a period of time after that, however, I didn't have faith; I had an empty box where my faith used to be.

Eventually, feeling as though I was hurting myself more than God, I became nostalgic for my robust prayer life. My first tentative prayers to God were in selfish gratitude for having this man back in my life. Before long I was back to praying for guidance and direction, solace, repentance, and a sense of connection to something larger than myself. While I have never fully reconciled with God for the pain and sorrow that my friend was put through (and probably never will), in other ways my connection with the Divine has never been deeper, more productive, or more dependable.

≈◯◯≈

God and I still have our moments, but I know that I am not alone in that. Many of us have been, are now, or will be, at some point, pissed at God. The reasons will vary: feelings of abandonment; the loss of a child, a spouse, or a mother or father; financial setbacks, the stock market crashing, or somebody looting your 401K plan; loneliness or natural disasters that wipe out hundreds of thousands of innocent bystanders; or lost opportunities (like Steve Johnson dropping a winning touchdown pass). Sometimes these feelings work themselves out on their own, but when our resentment toward God festers—which it often does when it goes unexpressed—that resentment can lead us to shut down a part of our souls. Without a spiritual road map back to the emotional Promised Land of peace and prosperity in faith, many people lose their relationship with God simply because they feel as though they do not have a right to quarrel, to demand answers, or to question, "My God, my God, why have you forsaken me?"

Judging by the venomous blowback Johnson got for daring to cry out "Why?" not everybody is ready for that kind of honest relationship with the Divine.

In the years that Exline has been studying prayer, angry prayer, and, in particular, angry prayer directed at God, her research indicates that we should not be surprised about the level of discomfort that exists on the subject. She tells me, "People may also be more comfortable admitting to milder feelings, such as disappointment or frustration, rather than coming right out and saying that they are angry at God." The notion of being mad at God is just too scary a proposition for some, so, Exline says, they are inclined to be euphemistic and to "describe a sense of spiritual dryness when they are actually suppressing anger.

"God might seem far away," she says in explaining this phenomenon, and "a person might not be all that interested in spiritual things or in trying to connect with God. Prayers might become a bit trite and predictable, with no depth of feeling, because there are big issues that are being swept under the rug. In this case anger toward God could become like *the elephant in the room*. Something that is actually very obvious but that believers may try to ignore in their conversations with God."

Exline's research concerning human/Divine anger also reveals some surprising data about the anger that atheists and agnostics have *regarding God* versus the anger they have *at God*. More on "the prayers of atheists" later.

So what's the message here? Like Steve Johnson, Moses, Job, Jesus, and yours truly, we all need to be honest with our feelings. Your prayers will be so much more meaningful and productive once you become comfortable with idea that God is okay with the full dimension of your human emotions.

What's next? Let's start with what anger is, why it's important to recognize it, and why it's okay to have it—to a point.

Chapter Two

WHAT IS ANGER, AND ISN'T IT ALWAYS BAD?

I know this to be true: If most people knew how to pro-cess their anger appropriately, we would never have any "good" reality TV shows. From profanity-riddled tirades on *The Real Housewives* series to fistfights on *Jersey Shore* to unhinged outbursts on *Dance Moms* (my personal favorite as of this writing), anger is front and center in our culture. Dr. Judith Orloff, psychiatrist, therapist, medical intuitive, and author of best-selling books including *Emotional Freedom: Liberate Yourself from Negative Emotions and Transform Your Life,* tells me, "We are in the midst of an emotional meltdown. Today, there is rage everywhere."

But why? What is making people so angry? What is amping up the level of *anger* to *rage*? Even with such tur-moil, is anger ever really an appropriate response? Ther-apist Dr. Les Carter, the author of *The Anger Trap: Free Yourself from the Frustrations That Sabotage Your Life,* who is known by many as "America's anger expert," says yes. In our interview, Carter says anger can be a perfectly appropriate response to an inappropriate situation if it is "good anger."

Regarding "good anger," Carter says that people sometimes need permission to express "the emotion of self-preservation, prompting the individual to stand up for personal worth, needs, and convictions." Carter encourages us to understand the importance of anger in maintaining reasonable emotional balance.

Unfortunately, Carter told me, the anger model that we see most often in popular culture is what he defines as "bad anger," that is, anger that tears down others and causes hurt because it is anger "displayed in an aggressive fashion with shouting, criticism, impatience, agitation, annoyance, irritability, and rudeness." Bad anger, like the kind that we witness most often on reality TV shows, can be frightening, and it should be. This is the kind of anger that will break up your marriage, damage your children, and get you fired (eventually) on *Celebrity Apprentice*.

"When you are in harmony with others, calmness and contentment are likely," explains Carter. "You *do* feel angry when disharmony is experienced, when others are dismissive, argumentative, insensitive, or rude. Anger taps into your need for self-preservation and that can be a good thing."

In this case, self-preservation does not necessarily refer to a life-or-death situation. We are self-preserving when we do not allow somebody else to define us negatively, for example, when we resist being told "you will never amount to anything" or "you are not a good person" or "you are unlovable." Taking a stand and defending yourself is the first step in not being disrespected by others, and that's why sometimes anger in its proper perspective is an appropriate, albeit a temporary, emotion, according to Carter.

"In anger you want to convey a message that your needs should be taken seriously and that you wish to be respected. Ideally, anger becomes the vehicle for getting the relationship back into harmony."

But if good anger is intended to be transformative and ultimately constructive in the name of peace, then "bad anger" occurs when anger is expressed without clean, understandable motives; it is ultimately destructive and has no perceivable positive outcome.

The classic story of Jesus cleansing the Temple, the war against Adolf Hitler and Nazi oppression, and the civil rights movement of the 1960s are all examples of righteous "good anger" in action intended to correct grave injustices. Whenever humans help bring order to a chaotic situation, we are doing God's work. As the expression goes, "No justice, no peace." Injustice loves complacency.

Let's look at another quick example of bad anger. A tired father comes home from a tough day of feeling disrespected at work. He yells at his kids for some imagined infraction just because it is his way of blowing off some steam. It may make him feel better temporarily, but there are repercussions—hurt feelings, arguing, and maybe even tears. Improving your own mood by ruining somebody else's is destructive, hurtful, and selfish. This kind of aggressive, caustic, humiliating outburst is the kind of anger that is referred to in the Seven Deadly Sins as wrath; it creates more injustice; it does not correct injustice.

But "non-aggressive anger" or "passive anger" should not be misunderstood as "good anger."

Passive anger is anger that is not expressed overtly and can be mistakenly construed as being better than "aggressive" anger because it is subtler and quieter. In actuality, passive anger and aggressive anger are two sides of the same coin. Typically, Carter says, people use

> aggressiveness in passive ways by giving the silent treatment, being stubbornly noncooperative, or saying what the other person wants to hear then doing the opposite. Either way, the core message of self-preservation is sent in a manner that leaves the other person feeling rejected or invalidated. When you do this you are treating others with the very disdain that you are asking not be given to you. Likewise you are contributing to the very disharmony you presumably wish to eliminate.

"People committed to healthy anger use *assertiveness*," asserts Carter; "they will openly stand in preservation of their needs and worth, but in a manner that also upholds the dignity of the other person. Boundaries can be established, stipulations can be distinguished, and convictions can be clearly conveyed . . . all while communicating with a spirit of goodness and regard. And turnabout is fair play too since assertive people will show a willingness to hear the other's feelings and concerns without discounting them."

And once more, establishing this kind of authentic relationship with God proves to be similar to building an authentic relationship with any other person we can actually see. If we are seeking a real connection to God, then we need to be honest with our feelings, and our relationship must be grounded in reality in order for the relationship to work. Good, constructive anger, expressed cleanly and without hurtful motives, will keep the lines of communication flourishing and productive.

Carter sees evidence of the proper use of anger in the Letter of Saint Paul to the Ephesians:

> In one teaching passage (Ephesians 4:15, 4:26) the apostle Paul indicates that we can speak the truth in love and be angry without sin. Most people do not see love and anger as being on the same side of the page, but that is exactly what happens when you have clean motives. If you love someone, of course you will address problematic issues but you will be careful to do it constructively and with the same decency that you would like to receive.

In other words, do unto others as you would have them do unto you—especially when you're pissed as hell at them. The trick is learning to be assertive without being aggressive. Carter says:

> Perhaps the key to being assertive versus aggressive is that assertive people have enough inner peace that they can stand their ground when it is time to be self-preserving, but they can also discern when to be finished even when the other person does not respond maturely. Assertive anger requires a commitment to self-restraint.

Need a second opinion? Here's another way of looking at the duality of anger. Orloff concurs that we all need a little good anger from time to time, but she adds another stipulation: It's important to know when you're feeling anger and why. Unconscious anger, the kind that nurses ancient hurts and irritations, the kind that feeds a need for revenge and comes out when we may not even be aware of it, must be conquered, she told me. "Anger is healthy when you can consciously connect with it in yourself," Orloff says, "and have a choice about how you handle it—that is the definition of emotional freedom—rather than simply reacting and causing damage. Unconscious anger is dangerous and can hurt others irreparably and cause wars." Sometimes those wars are just skirmishes, like the conflict that erupted when Representative Joe Wilson of South Carolina yelled, "You lie!" at President Barack Obama during a speech to a joint session of Congress, or when Representative Michael Capuano of Massachusetts suggested that those interested in fighting for union rights take to the street and "get a little bloody . . . Nothing wrong with throwing a coffee cup at someone if you're doing it for human rights." Neither of them was joking, and neither shied away from admitting that their political frustrations had boiled over. Both men had to apologize for their comments and both minimized their anger as a "moment of passion."

This pattern is played out over and over in the media. A politician, a talk show host, or a celebrity explodes with ugly, violent rhetoric and then later tries to pass it off as simple "passion," almost as though they should be applauded for it.

Charlie Sheen verbally attacked his colleagues from the TV show *Two and a Half Men* in a series of televised rants. He said that producer Chuck Lorre was a "contaminated little maggot who can't handle my power and can't handle the truth." "Fools and trolls" supposedly surrounded the actor, but he reassured his audience, "If you're part of my family I will love you violently. If you infiltrate and try to hurt my family, I will murder you violently." After Charlie Sheen was fired and publicly ridiculed for his bizarre behavior, he tried to soften his image by later claiming, "I'm not angry, I'm passionate." After a long hiatus, Charlie Sheen returned to network television in *Anger Management*.

Of course, "anger" and "passion" are not synonymous. To be passionate means that you are suffering to some degree. Lashing out in anger means that very likely other people around you are suffering. Similarly, people with terrible tempers may be inclined to play down their anger as a personality trait that makes them "fiery" or "spicy."

For a few years, the fast-food chain Burger King even used "angry" to market spicy sandwiches like the "Angry Whopper" and the "Angry BK TenderCrisp Chicken Sandwich." In the process, the meaning of *angry* was further watered down, implying merely "flavorful." (I tried one of those "angry chicken sandwiches," by the way, and *angry* would be the perfect word to describe the reaction of my lower intestine afterward.)

Geraldo Rivera, Jerry Springer, and Maury Povich are among the daytime talk show hosts who built their ratings on angry guests and the angry audiences that love/hate them. There's even a new word for TV shows that are designed to get your blood boiling: Angertainment.

While we should understand that it's okay to express anger when it's appropriately self-preserving, we should always be aware of our anger, good and bad, passive and aggressive, conscious and unconscious, suppressed or not, be mindful of its power to hurt others, and never try to play up anger as something virtuous or as a trait absorbed from one's culture, that is, "Of course I'm fighting mad, I'm Irish."

On the opposite end of the spectrum, some ethnic groups seem to pride themselves on denying their anger. Having lived in Minnesota for many years, I have witnessed the Scandinavian cultural disapproval of displays of anger. I have known many people who confess to plastering on a smile to try to hide the cracks in their emotional state. While they may be artful in the sublimation of their anger, of course, they still feel it. They just suppress it.

Regardless of the reason, the harder we try to hold in anger without processing it in a healthy manner, the more it squishes out sideways in subtly destructive ways. Exline says, "Suppressed anger is a tricky thing. It can be bad for mental and physical health. There's an old expression that says, 'Depression is anger turned inward.'"

If Orloff is right when she says, "Today rage is everywhere," and if Exline is right when she says, "Depression is anger turned inward," perhaps that explains why American culture has never seemed so angry—and so dependent on antidepressants at the same time. So, before we move on, let's go over a quick checklist of how you can tell if you're experiencing feelings of anger—consciously or unconsciously. Does unconscious anger sound like a no-brainer? Well, not so much.

Psychologist and co-author of *Working with You Is Killing Me: Freeing Yourself from Emotional Traps at Work* Katherine Crowley says that whether you are observably losing your temper or doing a silent "slow burn" behind a phony smile or artificial patience, there are some telltale signs that you are angry.

"When a person experiences anger, his or her physiological system revs up. Adrenaline and noradrenaline surge through the body. Anger heats up more slowly in women than it does in men, but the bodies of both genders prepare for a fight," she told me.

"To the observer, an angry person usually shows anger in his or her face. The brow may furrow, teeth may clench, the individual may become flushed or pale. Some people clench their fists, others raise their voices, some may pound the table or throw something. Sweating, muscle tensions, and temperature changes are common."

Anger suppressors, those who feel anger but try to hide it, just make fists with their stomachs. "For these individuals," Crowley says, "anger may get stored in the abdomen, in the chest, in the neck and shoulders. An anger suppressor may feel irritated and uncomfortable, but won't seem visibly angry."

Do you see yourself in any of these descriptions? Is destructive or unexpressed anger damaging your relationships?

Now think about this. Are you angry with God? You might not be. That's fine. Plenty of us aren't. But when you pray, do you ever feel tense, frustrated, or uncomfortable? Could you write an awesome angry prayer right now off the top of your head?

That might just be a sign that there's something going on inside you that needs a little attention.

Chapter Three

ANGER MAKES YOU OLD; PRAYER KEEPS YOU YOUNG

Right now, I'm a little pissed at God. For all I know, God might be pissed at me too. Either way, God and I are not speaking to each other at the moment simply because once more I find myself lying on the floor of my home office with my laptop open, alternately trying to write and/or trying to fall asleep despite a horrendous, never-ending grinding noise in my ears. If tonight is like every other night, somehow before dawn I will end up doing a little writing and a little sleeping, but neither is coming easily tonight because of my deafening tinnitus.

Tinnitus is a largely irreversible condition that is characterized by irritating sounds like a "buzzing" or a "whistling" in the ears. Lucky me, I have *both*, a kind of "whistle buzz" for which there is as yet no cure. No one can hear it but me, of course, but it is present in every waking moment and most noticeable any time I try to sleep. If you can imagine having some invisible force hovering around your ear blowing a high-pitched buzzing whistle 24/7 then you have some idea about what it's

20

like to suffer from tinnitus. I know that I am in good company, though. Beethoven had it. Van Gogh had it. Look how uncrazy they turned out.

I prefer to think that the torture in my ears is not from God, but sometimes I'm not so sure. I prefer to believe that God is standing with me in my suffering, but, to borrow an expression, so far God has turned a deaf ear to my prayers for relief.

Yet I continue to pray, albeit sometimes through gritted teeth, because I believe that prayer always helps. My brain just works better when I keep it tuned with prayers and meditation. I'll get back to that thought, but first let's specify what prayer actually is and what it achieves. That's more ambitious than it sounds. There are as many different understandings of the purpose of prayer as there are organized religions in the world.

To put it simply, prayer is communication with the Divine. Sometimes that means talking, sometimes that means listening actively and intently for that still, small voice of God that mystics and sinners alike have spoken about for millennia. And if you're like me, prayer is a time to unleash your pains, your doubts, your desires, and your concerns because, well, I believe that God cares. According to some religious traditions, the faithful can and should petition God with lists of varying lengths of the things they hope God will fix—like a Divine "honey-do" list. Prayers need not be long, however. Some people pray for mere seconds but communicate a lot. When prayers are long, they often become a form of meditation.

Prayer is not always meditative, and meditation is not always prayerful. An easy way to tell the difference would be to say that prayers go outward to the Divine

and meditation goes inward to the self, but those defi-
nitions would be too easy to be true all the time. Unlike other kinds of prayer that attempt to go "outward"
toward the Divine, the goal of meditation is to train our
minds and bodies to become conscious of God not only
within us, but all around us.

Meditation is a form of communication that focuses
on neither active speaking nor active listening; it really
centers on being present, on being "in the moment," and
feeling what's moving you inwardly and what may be
pressing against you outwardly. For practitioners, meditation produces mental and physical clarity on many
levels but not always "lightning-bolt" moments. For example, a greater understanding of a problem may come
to you during meditation, but you may not realize it until
days later. Over time especially, meditation helps to open
us up to the Divine messages that come from all directions during our every waking and sleeping moment.

While the way people commune with the Divine var-
ies, ultimately, to some degree, we all end up in the same
place. Prayer makes us feel good. This brings us back to
why my brain just works better when I keep it tuned with
prayers and meditation: It's a medical fact—my brain,
your brain, everybody's brain functions at a higher level
whenever we pray and meditate.

After fifteen years of research, this is the scientific
conclusion of Dr. Andrew Newberg, M.D., an associate
professor of Radiology, Psychiatry, and Religious Studies at the University of Pennsylvania School of Medicine.
Newberg is a pioneer in the science of neurotheology,
a growing field that is defined as the study of the impact that faith has on the physical brain. Along with his
research assistants and co-author Mark Robert Wald-

man, Newberg has demonstrated consistently through thousands of brain scans of Jews, Christians, Muslims, Hindus, and New Age spiritualists—even agnostics and atheists—that whenever somebody contemplates God, however one perceives God, the human brain changes physically for the better.

Newberg confirmed in an interview what he detailed in his book *How God Changes Your Brain: Breakthrough Findings from a Leading Neuroscientist*, that when we pray and meditate on God and observe even simple spiritual, ritualistic practices, we "enhance the neural functioning of the brain in ways that improve physical and emotional health."

The prayer effect on our brains has both short- and long-term benefits. Newberg concludes that long-term, intense engagement with the Divine permanently restructures the part of our brain that controls mood, self-perception, and the way we look at the world. Ritual prayer (e.g., mantras, praying a Rosary, or using prayer beads) leads to increased peacefulness, social awareness, and a more compassionate worldview. In fact, Newberg's neurotheology research definitively indicates that a belief in and/or an active worship of God affects our brain positively.

But what happens to the faithful when they find themselves disconnected, angry, and unable to pray? The brain scans from Newberg's research are just as definitive. "People will lose their child or they will develop cancer and they will become angry with God and they will feel that God is no longer with them, they will have a crisis in their faith and, of course, when that does happen that does lead to negative consequences," Newberg explained to me. "When people have that kind of anger and fear, that turns on areas of our brain that foster negative emotions—e.g., being indiscriminately punitive, blameful, pessimistic—and releases stress hormones that literally have a damaging effect on the human body." Not surprisingly, retained, unprocessed anger's damaging effect on the human body is evident whether one is upset about a personal injustice or road rage, or mad that God appears to have cursed the Chicago Cubs. Newberg believes that suppressed anger wipes out all the positive effects on the brain that have occurred because of prayer. He claims, "There is a fair amount of evidence that shows that even when people are just struggling with their beliefs—what to believe and how to believe—that that can cause a great deal of stress and may even actually shorten their lives."

So the experts all agree: At some point in all of our lives, feelings of anger are inevitable and natural. It's not feeling anger that is the problem; the problem is not knowing healthy ways to process the anger in order to get to a place of peace again.

Keep your faith and live longer; lose your faith and die younger.

How about that for a lead-in to the next chapter?

Chapter Four

I'M PRETTY PISSED; CAN GOD REALLY HANDLE MY ANGER?

As we've established medically and psychologically, there is evidence that humans are designed to live longer and perform better with thoughtful, prayerful moments throughout the day. Furthermore, evidence suggests that we are hardwired to die younger and perform worse when we swap prayer time with time ruminating over bottled-up anger. While we are blaming and pointing our finger at the world, at others, and/or at God for any length of time, we're really holding a gun to ourselves. Literally, our repressed and/or unprocessed emotions hold us hostage.

Praying about the things that are truly angering us— including our hurt feelings, our frustrations, and our feelings of abandonment by God—means that we are establishing good boundaries. Just as it is proper to assert ourselves when we feel disrespected by others in our lives as a way of saying "I matter" to the person who may be hurting us, angry prayer toward God can mean standing up to God as a way of telling God that we matter too.

Granted, in human relationships, we may get more observable feedback than we get from the Almighty. Whether we talk it over or hug it out, whether it's tea and sympathy or a beer summit on the White House lawn, through effort and contact with each other it's possible for us (more or less) to get back to a place of peace and a sense of wholeness even when we feel hurt, confused, frustrated, or disrespected by the people with whom we are in conflict.

That's not as easy to do if you feel as if your whole world has been disordered by God, a Divine presence without eyes to meet our eyes or arms to hold us (or, for that matter, a beer to cheer us up). When something bad happens to me, anyway, it would be helpful if I could see "the face of God" while it's happening. While I am struggling in my life, is God giving me a knowing smile to let me know that it's all going to work out, or is God giving me a shrug of indifference? I can't see God so I can only guess. It's no wonder that people often feel confused as to the meaning of a life-changing event. A job has been lost, a child has been hit by a car, a teenager has committed suicide, a marriage vow has been broken—whatever the tragedy may be, it sure would be nice if belief didn't require so much faith.

"God never gives you more than you can handle" is the kind of bumper sticker theology that, in my experience, hurts as many people as it heals. Part of what bugs me about that expression is that it assumes that people who are experiencing more tragedy in their lives have, in a way, brought this hardship upon themselves because they are so strong. In this view, if God is giving us only what we can handle, it would seem to pay to be weak.

Another implication of the expression is that human

beings are exempt from responsibility for some of their own self-created tragedies. Sometimes we have only ourselves to blame for the bad things that are happening to us. Getting fired because you showed up drunk at the office falls into a different category than being fired from a job despite years of hard work and dedication. Sometimes bad things happen to good people; sometimes good people do stupid stuff with major consequences that should not be blamed on anybody but themselves.

On the occasion when bad things are happening to good people through no fault of their own, it's rare to meet somebody who is raised to express their anger easily to God. Many of us who were brought up in traditional religious households were taught that the only time we should ever raise our voices to God is in songs of praise. To do anything else, we are taught, would be blasphemy, right?

Yet over the years I've met a few enlightened men and women—Catholics, Protestants, Jews—who have absolutely no problem handing it to God in prayer when their worlds are crashing down around them. Journalist and Twin Cities pastor Rabbi Chaim Goldberger explains that in Judaism there is a certain peace with being in conflict with God because God is more than just the source of all good in our lives. "If you have a religion that teaches that God is the source of all good, how can you argue with good?" he asks. "Judaism has never taken that position. Our position is that God is the source of *everything*—good and evil—and that evil ultimately has a good purpose (even if) it hits us as evil." So, Rabbi Goldberger says, if you're getting hit with evil, and the evil is coming from God, it's your right to take your dispute back to the source in prayer.

But if challenging God through an angry prayer is always our right, does that mean that it is never wrong? Not exactly, explains Rabbi Goldberger: "The idea is that a person should be able to overcome his anger. But if you overcome your anger by not being real about it then that is also not right. The Talmud says that a person who gets angry is like somebody who is worshipping idols." Stay angry for a long period of time, harbor resentment and irritation, and you're worshipping idols to the tenth power.

This permission to *be real* when angry is grounded in the traditional Judeo-Christian belief that humans have been given an array of emotions by God. Anger is one of those God-given emotions, but, says Rabbi Goldberger, "it's a waste of the gift if you're walking around all day being angry about everything. Instead, in Judaism, the proper way to express any emotion is to take the middle road. For example, one shouldn't be too overly excitable but not too dull either." According to Rabbi Goldberger, Maimonides, the legendary twelfth-century Spanish rabbi, had a special place for the God-given emotion of anger. "For Maimonides," Rabbi Goldberger says, "anger is a little bit different. Maimonides believed you should feel just enough anger to have it never be said that you don't care about anything."

Another way to put that, perhaps, is that if you aren't mad about something, you're probably not paying attention.

Dr. Kenneth Hanson, a professor of Judaic Studies at the University of Central Florida, says expressing anger to God for the problems of the world is natural, and the more we embrace that anger, the more we can learn from it.

"I often talk about the 'two pillars' of Israelite monotheism," Hanson wrote to me. "(1) God is all-powerful (absolutely nothing happens in the universe that God doesn't control and ordain), and (2) God is all-just (everything that happens conforms to the Divine will). This puts the monotheist on the horns of a huge dilemma, for he now has to explain every terrible thing that happens to everybody on earth.

"How to pray when you're pissed at God," Hanson says, "is a major subject for my classes but it's taught as literature.

"The most important theme we address is the idea that the dominant school in ancient 'wisdom literature' advocated a hard-headed, nuts-and-bolts approach to life, not unlike the Greek stoic philosophers. But there was a smaller group, call them *subversives*, restless spirits who refused to be satisfied with pat answers. Often angry at the seeming brittleness of monotheism, they were responsible for a new level of spiritual depth that had never been seen before—namely—being 'pissed at God' and occasionally others is an essential step toward higher spirituality."

Hanson confirms, "God can take our anger. In Judaism, there's no prohibition about questioning God or the Divine will. On the contrary, one is supposed to question everything. The individual sheets of parchment on any Torah scroll are sewn together with threads from the thigh/sinew part of a kosher animal, to remind the worshipper that when Jacob wrestled with an angel/ God, he was struck lame in his thigh. But he also became 'Israel.' In other words, every time one approaches the Bible, one is expected to have a wrestling match with God. Cool, huh?"

Cool, indeed.

Trusting that God can take our anger, we may adapt our approach to other circumstances when we are not mad at God per se but may want to use our prayers to vent about others. For example, in San Salvatore, a fifteenth-century Italian church, a group of Franciscan friars was frustrated at the number of Bibles that were being stolen by visitors. Here in this sacred landmark that has been attracting tourists since Michelangelo made it one of his favorite stops, the Franciscan monks were heartbroken when a rare and expensive Bible was pilfered directly from the church's lectern.

When a replacement Bible provided by a worshipper also went missing within a few days of its being placed in the sanctuary, the friars had finally had enough. So right there, on display for tourists and worshippers to see, the monks prayed openly in a posted sign for the thief to repent and return the Bibles. Short of that, the monks said, it was their hope that the perpetrator be afflicted by God with a massive case of diarrhea.

In fact, the Franciscan friars' exact language was, "We pray to God that the thief is struck by a strong bout of shits."

According to the Italian newspaper *La Stampa*, a public prayer of anger directed at a thief may not sound orthodox, but it is consistent with the Tuscan love of irony.

"It is not exactly clean language," a friar said, "but we couldn't put up with it any longer. The Lord and the faithful will understand."

I think the Lord understood that prayer even before the monks posted it, and it fits in perfectly with dozens of prayers in the Bible that implore God to do much worse things to people. Believe it or not, not only are there some pretty raw prayers in the Bible that few people talk about, but the dirty little not-so-secret secret of biblical translators is that God uses the Hebrew rough equivalent of the f-word in anger as quoted by the prophet Jeremiah. That might take a minute or so to sink in, so I'll save that for a later chapter. Startling? As Franciscan monks might say, it's not exactly clean language, but God couldn't put up with it any longer.

In the end, love and anger can be on the same side of the page, and learning to express our anger cleanly to each other and to God will build a better relationship. The measure of success in any relationship should never be whether you have ever said words in anger, but rather that your words were not meant to be cruel, you truly meant what you said, and you were able to share your perspective constructively.

Prayers like "We pray to God that the thief is struck by a strong bout of the shits" may seem crazy, but from time to time maybe we all have to lose our mind a little to find our faith. This was never truer in my own experience than early in my first semester as a chaplain intern. What happened that day forever changed the way I would pray in the future.

Chapter Five

ANGRY PRAYER AT WORK

*I don't think of myself as somebody with a lot of God-*given talents, but if I had to list one it would be that I am not squeamish around medical procedures. For example, I was allowed to scrub up and watch both of my wife's C-sections. Horror movies with a lot of fake blood don't interest me, but I could watch real surgeries with real blood all day long. In a traditional church environment the ability to be comfortable around bodily fluids goes largely unused. In a hospital, however, it's like a super-power.

Being at ease in a hospital setting has allowed me to learn some of the greatest life lessons, such as "If you can't say it while looking into the eyes of somebody who is dying then chances are it's not true." In my service as a chaplain intern, and then later as a deacon working in various churches, I was privileged to counsel men and women who were straddling the line between life and death. Most of the time that kind of duty requires being a good listener and is best described as a "ministry of presence."

While I was a chaplain intern in a large, Southern, urban hospital, I was asked to check in on a family that had gathered in an unused hospital room. A teenager was in a coma in the Pediatric Intensive Care Unit (PICU), and his chances of survival were not good. The hospital allowed his extended family to use this unoccupied room for a couple days so that they could be near him around the clock. I had not been told much about the situation beforehand. I knew that there had been a farm accident of some type, that the family was evangelical Christian, and that their minister had already stopped by the hospital. I wasn't sure what I could do, but I went in if only to offer the services of the hospital's Pastoral Care Office.

I knocked on the door and some friendly, smiling voices welcomed me. I entered to find that the hospital room had been converted into a family command post. The shades were pulled back; the furniture had been rearranged to make it cozy. One table had been pushed to the wall, and spread out on it was a buffet of chips, M&Ms, healthy snacks, and several two-liter bottles of pop. Chairs had been arranged with one of the beds to form a kind of prayer circle.

Around the circle of chairs were three well-dressed, neatly coiffed, fortyish women with Bibles in their laps.

"Hello, my name is Ian, and I am the chaplain on the floor today."

"Hello, pastor," they said, giving me too much credit. "C'mon in and sit down."

"Well, I'm not a pastor yet, but I am a seminary student, and I am here to see how I might be of service to you."

"You could come and pray for us and keep praying for

33

our nephew," said one of the ladies sadly. We all introduced ourselves, and they told me that two of them were
the blood kin of this young accident victim—we'll call
him "Jimmy"—and the other was a family friend who
was all but related. They all lived near each other, went
to church together, and had traveled up from the southern part of the state after Jimmy had been airlifted to the
hospital's pediatric trauma unit.

Just a day before, Jimmy had been riding his motocross
motorcycle around the farm when he hit something, flew
forward, and the bike landed on top of him. His skull
had been fractured in a couple places. The impact literally shifted his brain inside his skull, and doctors thought
it best to induce a coma because of swelling and a fear
that brain death could occur. If he lived, the family had
been told that permanent brain damage was a likely possibility.

After Jimmy was flown to the hospital, his entire family was mobilized. Within a short time family members
were notified, prayer groups were initiated, bedside vigil
schedules were organized, thermoses were filled with
coffee, food was brought to the hospital, and caravans of
visitors were formed that went to and from the hospital.
This boy's family moved like a well-drilled platoon into
their new hospital headquarters where, armed with their
faith and spearheaded by Jimmy's aunts, these steel mag-
nolias in hair-spray helmets were determined to pray this
boy into a full recovery.

A group of close family members had spent the night at
the hospital, but the aunts were about to rotate out from
the front lines to go back to the community 150 miles
away and bring in reinforcements. Their home church
pastor had been present all morning. By the way they

spoke about him you could tell he held a special place of respect with them. As far as they were concerned, he was famous, so the ladies asked if I knew their small-town minister.

"No, I'm afraid I don't know many of the pastors outside of metro," I told them, "but I would love to meet him. It sounds like you're in very good hands." They all smiled and told me how great the pastor had been to be there praying with them, and how Jimmy was going to have a total healing, they "just knew it." It was all going to be fine.

Just fine. Really, fine. Soon. Fine.

But those assurances seemed forced, and judging by their nervous, quick smiles I sensed doubt and frustration. It seemed to me that under their calming exterior these women were holding something back.

"Are there any questions you would like to ask me?" I asked.

One of the women looked sort of blankly at me, one shook her head for a little "no," but the third lady opened the door a bit when she just said quietly, "Well . . ."

So I started with her. "What would that be?" I asked.

"Well, I don't understand why this is happening," she said.

"You mean, how could God let this happen to Jimmy?" I replied.

"Yes, how could this happen to a sweet boy like Jimmy?"

After that, the conversational floodgates opened. Not surprisingly, it was as if all three women had been thinking to themselves about where God was in this accident but were afraid to be the first one to say anything out loud for fear of what the others might think.

Amongst theologians and great Scrabble players, the question of God's presence in the face of an evil or tragic event is summed up by the word *theodicy*, which comes to English from the German version of a Greek word for "God order." More than just pondering why "bad things happen to good people," theodicy goes to the core of the religious experience: Where is my all-knowing, all-loving God now?

"Pastor, do you think it was the devil who did this to Jimmy?" asked the oldest aunt.

But one of the other ladies answered even before I could: "Darlin', if God is all-powerful, then God had to let the devil do this to Jimmy! And that just doesn't seem right."

Then after much lively but inconclusive conversation, one aunt summed it up best when she said, "It's just been so hard to pray to a God that I'm mad at!"

I asked, "So why can't you pray to God about how angry you are?"

After a brief silence there was a little nervous laughter before one of the aunts confessed, "It just seems so . . . I mean, who am I to question God?"

Another aunt added, "Just doesn't sound like something Jesus would do."

And so I asked them to open their Bibles to Psalm 22 and to take turns in the circle reading aloud. If you have never read Psalm 22, trust me when I say that despite the obtuse biblical metaphors, the ancient symbolism, the sometimes awkward figures of speech, the distinct wail of somebody feeling abandoned by God was heard by the aunts.

It starts like this:

My God, my God, why have you forsaken me?
Why are you so far from helping me, from the words
    of my groaning?
O my God, I cry by day, but you do not answer,
and by night, but find no rest.

Later in Psalm 22, however, the references start to get a little obscure for the modern reader:

Many bulls encircle me,
strong bulls of Bashan surround me;
they open wide their mouths at me,
like a ravening and roaring lion.

I am poured out like water,
and all my bones are out of joint;
my heart is like wax;
it has melted within my breast;
my mouth is dried up like a potsherd,
and my tongue sticks to my jaws;
you lay me in the dust of death.

After reading aloud in a circle for several minutes, despite the occasional raised "What does that mean?" eyebrow, these women were rejuvenated by the psalmist's example of an authentic, dimensional, emotionally mature, personal relationship with God that doesn't have to be limited to prayerful pleasantries. We all felt a thick moment of freedom. We put away our Bibles and had a good, honest freestyle prayer for Jimmy, the kind where everybody just said exactly what was on their mind and let go of any worry of whether it was "churchy" enough.

So how is this an example of angry prayer in action? Well, the aunts' anger toward a God they felt had abandoned them evaporated after they expressed their feelings. Like a geyser at Yellowstone National Park, sometimes things build up and they have to come out. If those feelings don't come out, people explode or everything emotional just comes squishing out sideways. After praying about how angry they were, the aunts told me later, they continued to pray without reservation.

Still, remembering how frustrated we all were with the sometimes bumpy, archaic language of Psalm 22 when we read it around the prayer circle in their hospital headquarters, it became a kind of "Here I stand" moment for me. Thinking about how important the anger expressed in Psalm 22 had been to these ladies and how it seemed to give them permission to express themselves more freely, I began researching the psalms further and telling people's stories by rewriting the angriest, most frustrated, pain-filled psalms in the Bible so that the truth of their emotion and the permission of their prose could be more accessible to other patients with whom I came in contact in my rounds as a chaplain intern and later as a pastor.

Before I went home at night, I would sit next to Jimmy in PICU and work on my rewording of Psalm 22 while he slumbered in his coma. Although I never shared it with the aunts, this is what I came up with:

AN ANGRY PRAYER FOR
SOMEBODY FEARING FOR THEIR LIFE

My God, my God, why have you forsaken me?
Why are you so far from helping me?
Don't you hear my pain?
God, I cry out to you by day.

Nothing happens. By night? Silence.
My parents and my ancestors believed in you
and you helped them—
I've heard the stories.
So why not me? What did I do?
My family has cried out to you and they were saved!
Lots of people I know have trusted you, God,
and you didn't let them down.

So to you I must be a worm and not a human,
a nonhuman to be scorned and despised by you
as I am by others.
Because it's not like my faith is helping my social
      standing either, God.
It feels like everybody who sees me just mocks me.
They hurl insults because I'm so pathetic,
and they shake their heads saying:
"This idiot believes in God; let God help!
If God exists, let God prove it by helping this loser."

But since the day I was born, I have been yours.
You made me trust in you even while I was nursing!
From my mother's womb you have been my God.
So now—when I need you the most—why are you
      so far away?

HOW TO PRAY WHEN YOU'RE PISSED AT GOD

Do you know what this feels like?
God, it's like I am being chased down the street
by some psycho guy in a scary truck determined to
*   run me over.*
Sweating and breathless and in fear for my life,
I jump over a backyard fence to escape,
only to discover that I'm now surrounded by
*   starving, snarling pit bulls.*
I'm trapped.

Bite by bite, God, life is killing me.
I'm spent and physically I'm so exhausted
that all my bones are out of joint.
My heart has turned to wax and melted away
*   within me.*

God, I need to be refreshed so badly;
I need a streak of things to go right.

Imagine me as a clay flower pot that has been
*   smashed*
on a hot, sunny patio.
No matter how much water you pour on those
*   broken pieces,*
that pot cannot hold water anymore.
That's me. My soul is so parched;
my tongue sticks to the roof of my mouth.
Like that broken pot, I have been laid down for a
*   dusty death,*
baking in the hot sun, useless.
Imagine that, God!
The pit bulls are getting closer,
their bites are going deeper,
and that psycho guy in the truck is driving

*around the block faster and faster looking
    for me,*
and I've got nothing in reserve.

The dogs have now pierced my hands and my feet,
and it feels like there is no way out.
I am wasting away from my wounds,
and I know that people can tell.
*They stare and whisper to themselves as I pass on
    the street,*
and I'm sure some people think it's funny
and that I deserve this somehow.
*So-called friends are already taking advantage of my
    weakness*
*and can't wait to get their hands on my small
    treasures.*
Like jackals they are licking their chops,
*waiting for me to drop so that they can divide up
    what I have earned.*

*So, O Lord, O my Strength, come quickly to
    help me*
for I'm having trouble hanging on.
Deliver me from this cutting pain,
*my precious life from the vicious power of that
    which is tearing me apart!*
Make me invisible to those who seek to hurt me;
*make those who want to profit off my pain forget
    my name and where I live.*
*In exchange, I will raise your name to my brothers
    and sisters;*
in the congregation I will praise you.
You who respect the power of the Lord, praise God!

For God has heard the suffering of this afflicted one.
God has not hidden from my cry for help.
At least somebody has listened!

The poor will eat and be satisfied;
those who seek the Lord will praise God—
may their hearts live forever.

All the ends of the earth will remember
and turn to the Lord in their pain,
for God will listen
even when my family and friends are sick of hearing
*   about my problems!*
No matter where you are in the world,
God will share in your pain.
People will speak of God even on their deathbed,
and generations will proclaim God's righteousness
to a people not yet born—
that's how cool God is. Amen.

∞◯◯◦

One night a while later I was praying with Jimmy, who was still in a coma, when one of his specialists came in and (as doctors are permitted to do with chaplains) we talked about the boy's chances for returning to his old life. The doctor talked in low percentages about Jimmy's physical and mental recovery. The odds of total recovery still weren't good, he thought, but the next couple of days were going to be crucial. The brain swelling was going down and they were going to let him come out of the coma. If Jimmy responded well to various stimuli, the doctor would be hopeful, but he didn't expect much. Despite being somewhat of a cynic about religion, he told me, the doctor encouraged me to keep praying. If nothing else, he thought, it was helping the family stay positive, and that made it easier for him to talk to them.

A few days later I got the word we'd all been hoping for: Jimmy was awake enough to move his eyes back and forth and wiggle his toes. Tears ran sideways down his face when he saw his mother by his side. It was apparently quite a scene.

I saw the boy only one more time, when the family was transferring him out of PICU into a regular pediatric room. Purely by accident, I got off an elevator and bumped into the aunts as Jimmy's parents were wheeling him down the hallway to his new digs.

His parents stopped the hospital bed in the hallway and introduced me to their now fully awake son. Holding his hand steady, I told Jimmy how proud I was of him and reminded him how lucky he was to have so many people who loved him. Jimmy still couldn't say much, but there was a lot of relief and dismay on his rugged, bruised, and battered face. Looking back, it would have been beneficial to have Newberg's brain scans of Jimmy's family while their prayers were all bottled up and then afterward when the conversation with God was flowing freely again. Perhaps there would have been evidence of a theory I have that angry prayers are an ancient, necessary tool to help restore order to internal chaos in tragic times. Spiritually, emotionally, psychologically, mentally, physically, we're always better off when we start our recovery by naming our unhappiness to God.

And why shouldn't we? I've never quite understood people who profess a faith in an all-knowing, all-loving God who think that if they just "pray nice" then God will never know how pissed they really are.

Chapter Six

SERIOUSLY, WHY HAVE YOU FORSAKEN ME?

I admit, I tend to see the mystical in what other people may find merely coincidental. For example, did you know that "The righteous shall inherit the land, and live in it forever" is a sentence that appears similarly in the Hebrew Bible, the Christian Bible, *and* the Qur'an (Psalm 37:29 and Surah 21:105)? Given that the same line appears in so many copies of holy books, it seems as if it is God/Allah's way of saying *righteousness* (a state of integrity, wholeness, uprightness) really, really, really matters.

Which is not to suggest, by the way, that Muslims find anger toward God permissible. According to my friend Dr. David Penchansky, professor of theology at St. Thomas University in St. Paul, Minnesota, and author of *Understanding Wisdom Literature: Conflict and Dissonance in the Hebrew Text*, Muslim theology makes no room for a book like this. Penchansky was born Jewish, converted to the World Assemblies of God Fellowship after spending some time at a commune in the 1970s, then converted to Catholicism as a student on the way to earning his Ph.D. Penchansky teaches on Semitic languages and ancient texts, and his interest in Islam and Arabic expanded after he married a Muslim woman he met in the United States and after he spent many (very hot) summers with her family in Saudi Arabia. Penchansky cautions in an interview:

> For Muslims, and in the Qur'an, it is inconceivable that one would offer an angry prayer to God. That would be regarded as disrespectful and blasphemous. Although there is much overlap between many Bible stories and the Qur'an, all of the places that one finds angry prayers in the Bible are not found in the Qur'an, not even a trace. Although Job is mentioned, the idea (as in traditional Christian interpretation) is that Job is faithful in his suffering and God rewards his faithfulness. In fact, when I show Muslims the angry prayers in the Bible, they see this as evidence of the inferiority of the Bible and evidence of its corruption.

Anyway, it may be more mystical thinking on my part, but I also think it's significant that Psalm 22— one of the least known, least understood psalms—is in the Bible right next to the Twenty-third Psalm, the best known, most quoted, most loved psalm in human history ("The Lord is my shepherd, I shall not want . . ."). The Twenty-third Psalm poetically praises God for being so trustworthy, even when we stand before the gates of hell; Psalm 22 challenges God by saying, "Where the hell are you?" There are many "praise psalms" in the Bible, but there are even more psalms of anger, lament, and fear.

And even though unhappy psalms share the same pedigree, the same authorship, the same history as other prettier psalms—and despite being written to be performed and sung just like the Twenty-third Psalm and the other more popular biblical songs—they go virtually ignored even by the most avid Bible readers and congregations except on rare occasions.

In fact, because the psalms of anger, lament, and fear are laced with so much suspicion toward God, most Christians completely turn away from them. While there are exceptions, many people are uncomfortable with these "Prayers for the Pissed Off" because they explore the unsatisfied, distrustful side of the faithfuls' committed relationship to the Divine and question head-on whether perhaps there are times when an all-knowing, all-loving God just does not care about us at all.

And yet Psalm 22 has another component that is worth mentioning, one that came into play for me toward the end of my first rotation in PICU, a story that bookends Jimmy's recovery and illustrates another aspect of how angry prayer works.

"Nathan" was a young boy who was not in a good place. This kid had a very severe case of a blood disease, and he had become a regular visitor to the PICU. He was twelve, but because of his health setbacks Nathan was small for his age. His mother was the one who had asked for a visit from a chaplain. When I came into the room, she was there knitting in the corner in a rocking chair, a large woman with huggy arms, a big smile, and a warm personality, but, as I was to discover, in calling for a chaplain she had an agenda.

"Oh, I am so glad you are here! This is my son, Nathan, and, pastor, he just told me today that he no longer believes in God! Can you believe it? We've got our whole church praying for him, and Nathan says he doesn't believe in God and he doesn't want the prayers! Pastor, you have got to help me! I told him he'll never get well unless he gets right with the Heavenly Father!"

While his mother was talking, I was keeping an eye on the boy's reactions to her words and tone. Judging by Nathan's subtle eye rolls, he had been hearing that message a lot from his mom lately. Of course, she had reason to want a miracle. She was a single mother, the sole income earner with two other kids at home. It took an understanding boss and two buses for her to come see Nathan every day, and he was not improving as the doctors had hoped. Nathan was in a statistical group of children whose anemia might even become fatal.

I asked her permission to spend some time with Nathan alone. She agreed, said good-bye to us, and headed home to make dinner for her other kids. Before she left, however, she gave me one of those "mom looks" and told me she was counting on me to "bring this boy back to God." I detected no excitement from the patient in the hospital bed at this possibility.

I wish I could say that as soon as his mom left the room Nathan's demeanor changed and he began to share his every thought. Instead, he stared out the window as I talked. He did roll his head in my direction from time to time, and that seemed promising, so I started asking some simple questions. At first he didn't make eye contact as he answered.

"How long has this been going on?" I started.

"I forget."

"Other than dorks like me bugging you, what do you hate most about the hospital?"

"I miss my friends," he said quietly. "I miss playing with my friends."

"Tell me about your friends."

"Terrell, T-Ball, and No-Say."

"There has got to be a story behind No-Say," I said.

"Yeah." He smiled. "His name is Jose, but he never says anything so we call him 'No-Say.' Good ballplayer."

"I bet you were a good ballplayer. What's your favorite sport?"

"Football. I miss football. I miss my friends."

"You had some moves."

"Used to. Someday."

"Do your friends ever come around to see you in the hospital?"

Nathan shook his head no. "Once." A moment later he shook his head again at some thought that he didn't share with me.

"Is that the hardest thing about being in the hospital?"

Nathan shook his head no again and looked out the window. "Needles."

"You hate getting stabbed with needles all the time?"

"I hate needles."

"I'm sorry. That must be so hard. Is there anything I can do?"

"Tell my mom I don't want to pray anymore." On this Nathan looked me dead in the eye. It really caught me off guard. While his mother was counting on me to "bring this boy back to God," Nathan needed me to help him get his mom off his back about prayer. It seemed like he was demanding respect for a boundary, but I was not sure if it was more of a boundary with God or his mom.

The more we talked, the clearer it got. He missed playing outdoors—running, climbing, bike riding—"kid world." A life-and-death struggle with a blood disease was no fun at all. No fun equaled "adult world." The kid world was about hanging with Terrell, T-Ball, and No-Say, while the adult world was about doing what the doctors told him to do, swallowing nasty things, and always needles, needles, needles. For Nathan, needles had come to symbolize the difference between the never-ending, painful drudgery of the adult world and the ever-elusive joy of the kid world. Every stab of the needle reminded Nathan how little power he had over his life.

So where was the "Heavenly Father" that Nathan's mother so wanted me to help him "get right with" in any of that? I understood why Nathan was so sad, and it just got worse when I started asking questions about his earthly father. Nathan's dad was drunk and living on the streets. Nathan hardly ever saw him except sometimes from the window of the bus on his way to school.

It would be fair to say that for Nathan, the Heavenly Father was the same as this boy's earthly father—both absent for all intents and purposes. His little brother and sister were too young to remember a time when their father had been around much, but Nathan remembered, and he felt abandoned by his dad just when he needed him most.

Which is why it irked Nathan when his mom always referred to God as "Heavenly Father" in her prayers of thanksgiving at Nathan's bedside. Why did he have to thank God for being locked up in a hospital on a beautiful day when other kids were out playing? Why did God deserve to be praised at all? If God was so great, Nathan wondered, how come he himself was doing all the painful stuff? Why didn't God just make the pain go away? If God could send him back to the kid world, he would be a believer. Nathan would thank God and do a little "Praise Jesus" touchdown dance every time he scored if God would just get him out of the hospital.

Before Nathan turned away from prayer, he told me, one of the things he used to pray for was a visit from his dad, who never came. In his mind, God the Father and Nathan's father had been conflated as just one big disappearing act. If God was anything like his dad, Nathan knew better than to count on God.

As a result, his mother's prayers had become like the nurse's needles—one more painful routine that was supposed to be good for him.

Following the protocol of the chaplain program, I made a mental note to suggest a visit from one of the hospital's psychotherapists, but I also saw an opportunity both to honor his mother's request to minister to Nathan spiritually and to respect his pain.

Going back to my first couple of days in PICU, I remembered something that I had never brought up to Jimmy's aunts about Psalm 22, something that I thought a twelve-year-old boy would enjoy. The psalm has a kind of "secret code" in it.

"Hey, Nathan, before I go, would it be okay for me to teach you something from the Bible that even your mother probably doesn't know?"

As I suspected, that got his attention. He kind of smiled.

"Goes like this: '*Eloi, Eloi, lama sabachthani.*' Try repeating that with me," I said, and he did. It only took a few tries before Nathan was pronouncing it like a pro.

"Now, here's what '*Eloi, Eloi, lama sabachthani*' means. In the Bible, when Jesus is being crucified, feeling the pain of ten thousand needles, feeling forgotten by his friends and abandoned by God his Father, those were the exact words that Jesus spoke in the language that was commonly spoken at the time, Aramaic.

"And do you know what Jesus was yelling to God? 'My God, my God, why have you forsaken me?'"

Nathan's eyes widened a bit. His head cocked as he was considering what I was telling him.

As I had hoped, those words seemed to resonate with Nathan. I continued: "Jesus does not say, 'Hey, God, this is going great, and I'm really grateful to be going through this torture.' Basically, Jesus yelled at his Heavenly Father, 'This stinks! Why don't you make the pain go away?'"

Nathan just nodded and said softly, "*Eloi, Eloi, lama sabachthani.*"

"Now, here's something even more amazing. When Jesus said, '*Eloi, Eloi, lama sabachthani,*' he was quoting the first line of Psalm 22, which is in one of the oldest parts of the Bible. Psalm 22 is not a happy prayer; it's a prayer of pain that is calling on God to step up and help us, asking God not to be so far from us in our time of groaning. It's an angry prayer, Nathan, and it's in the Bible. Know what that means?"

"No."

"That it's okay to be angry, and it's okay to be angry when you're praying to God."

As I remember it, Nathan just said, "Huh."

"When Jesus needed God to hear him most, he said '*Eloi, Eloi, lama sabachthani.*' When you need God to hear you most, Nathan, if you say that, God will hear you too."

I made no promises that Nathan would be transported miraculously to the nearest playground, just that he would feel that he was being heard.

I was gone from the hospital for a few days after that, but when I got back to our next regular clinical pastoral education meeting, there were a couple of messages waiting for me from Nathan's mom. Nathan had forgotten the exact Aramaic phrase, and it was really bothering him that he could not remember it.

I came to learn that after our first visit, each time somebody had to stab him with a needle, Nathan had found strength in saying *"Eloi, Eloi, lama sabachthani"*— sometimes right into the face of the nurse who was sticking him. His mom said that when Nathan had forgotten the exact words, he felt like he had lost his ability to speak truth to power!

When I visited Nathan again that afternoon, I wrote it down for him and dog-eared the page where he could find it in the Bible (Mark 15:34). I even got to see Nathan use it once to a nurse who was drawing blood from his needle-weary little arm.

"Eloi, Eloi, lama sabachthani," he deadpanned to her when she finished.

"I'm so sick of that," the nurse said under her breath as she turned to leave, and Nathan and I cracked up. It wasn't much, perhaps, but through a little bit of angry prayer, Nathan had established some of the boundary he was craving. He might have to live in the "adult world" a while longer, but that plea became his private code between him and God.

That day I shared with Nathan and his mother my rewriting of Psalm 22, the one that I had originally done for Jimmy and his aunts. I did not know how Nathan's mom would react, but I thought Nathan would like all the "horror movie" imagery. She really liked the part about the snarling pit bulls—she hated dogs—and hearing this version of the psalm helped Nathan's mom have a much clearer understanding of what Nathan was going through. The angry prayer worked to the extent that Nathan's mother knew that when she prayed "prayers of praise," those prayers were for her and her relationship with God. Nathan needed something else.

My CPE semester ended just a few days later, but before I left, some pastors connected to the area's homeless community secured Nathan a going-away present from me. Working through some street guys who knew Nathan's father, the pastors got a message to him about his son and what he was going through. Making sure Nathan's father knew where his son was and how much a visit from him would mean was all we could do. I do not know whether Nathan ever got a surprise visit, but I sure hope his earthly father stepped up. I pray his Heavenly Father did too.

Chapter Seven

THREE STEPS TO TAKE BACK
YOUR PRAYER LIFE

At the beginning of the book I wrote about Buffalo Bills wide receiver Steve Johnson, who was so upset after having bobbled what should have been a winning touchdown that he tweeted to God: "I praise you 24/7!!! And this is how you do me!!! You expect me to learn from this!! How?? I'll never forget this!! Ever!! Thx tho!"

Sports media, talk radio, and the majority of his Twitter followers reacted negatively to Johnson's proclamation, but I don't believe that God did. Johnson may have dropped the ball in the end zone, but, as I hope I have proven, he caught something righteous in those brief lines. In fact, his tweet is like a mini-anger psalm. Johnson told me personally that he was unaware of the structure of the Bible's angry prayers, yet he followed the classic biblical three-part model perfectly.

My former seminary professor, the Bible scholar Dr. Walter Brueggemann, is credited with first describing the three parts of the typical, distraught, plaintive biblical psalm as "orientation, disorientation, and reorientation." The "orientation" explains who the person is and what he or she is experiencing; the "disorientation" part focuses on how these experiences are disrupting the person's relationship with God, the world, their family, and so forth; and "reorientation"—and there usually is a reorientation in the Bible psalms but not always—confirms that God is in charge and expresses hope that things will be right again.

But at the risk of sounding disrespectful, in my experience Brueggemann's description needed improvement for use outside the ivy-covered walls of the seminary. In the chaplaincy of hospital rooms and church hallways, I found it quicker and easier to describe the three-part structure of the typical angry prayer as "name, proclaim, and reframe."

Let's use Johnson's tweet as a quick example of "naming it, proclaiming it, and reframing it."

"I praise you 24/7!!! And this is how you do me!!!" Confrontational at the beginning, Johnson affirmed his love of God and then went right into his feeling of abandonment. That "old buddy" familiarity with God that Johnson expressed reflects the depth and clarity of his relationship with the Lord. He goes on to *proclaim*, "You expect me to learn from this!! How??" This is a legitimate question when one is suffering; it is a question that is proclaimed often in the psalms of the Bible. Of course, in any other place besides the twittersphere, the proclamation could go on until the person praying felt that he or she had gotten it all out of their system.

Johnson told me that the next proclamation—"I'll never forget this!! Ever!!"—is less about harboring a grudge for eternity and more about his reluctant awareness that he will be mulling over the meaning of this lesson from God for the rest of his life. It's indicative of his theology that we should learn from everything good or bad that happens to us.

Which is why the final words, "Thx tho!" belie the charge that his tweet was an insolent act of apostasy. Johnson said he was being entirely sincere when he wrapped up his tweet with gratitude. In the end, in 140 characters or fewer, Johnson had *reframed* his reaction to a national embarrassment and a personal disappointment from anger to gratitude. Explaining and owning his confusion cleared the air and allowed him to get back to a place of peace. He was confused and felt let down by God, so he *named* his situation in a tweet, *proclaimed* his pain loudly, and then felt sufficiently cleansed to *reframe* the event as a positive one for which he could be grateful.

This then is the classic three-step cathartic purpose of angry prayer, indeed, the hope of counselors, therapists, and pastors everywhere. Convert our negative emotions and psychological roadblocks into something spiritually and mentally beneficial. And it all begins with the mature identification of what is hurting us, being able to express those feelings in a useful, clarifying manner, and then being able to let it go even if that means letting go a little bit at a time.

Of course, just like the directions on a bottle of shampoo—lather, rinse, repeat—in order to reframe our pain completely, emotional cleansing might need to take place over a period of time. One should not expect instant results, but there will be progress. Anybody who has ever tried to lose weight knows that the first pounds that one puts on are the last pounds to come off.

One tip? Sometimes brutal honesty might require

some brutal language, but I encourage you to refrain from being too self-conscious about that. God knows, sometimes when people are angry, things get said that would never be repeated in polite company. But good therapy is rarely about things that could be said in polite company, and an effective therapeutic angry prayer is no different. Besides, you'd be shocked by some of the curse words you could find in the Bible already if you knew where to look for them!

For example, the Bible warns against condemning people, cursing, and using coarse language, but the Bible itself is full of condemnations of people, cursing, and coarse language, almost always in anger. In Philippians 3:8, to be specific, Paul uses a Greek word, *skubalon*, that should properly be translated in English as "crap," or possibly "shit," but is most often passed off as "rubbish" or "garbage" due to the perception that the typical Bible reader would be offended. There are other Greek words Paul could have used if he had been worried about offending people, but instead he used *skubalon* as a coarse comparison, much in the way a modern person might when trying to make a similar point today. The passage could read like this:

> More than that, I regard everything as loss because of the surpassing value of knowing Christ Jesus my Lord. For his sake I have suffered the loss of all things, and I regard them as crap, in order that I may gain Christ.

Is *skubalon* really that big a deal even in this context? Paul never apologizes for writing so explicitly, and I think that's something worth remembering for people who feel restricted in what they think they can say to

God in prayer. Paul said what he meant, and, at least in Greek, he meant what he said.

I am confident that the more you know the Bible, the less self-conscious you will be in the words you choose for your angry prayers. You may be the kind of person who has never sworn in your life, but if praying truthfully requires you to use words, ideas, expressions, whatever, that have never passed your lips before, don't hold back. If that's what it takes for you to process your anger and to reconnect to the Divine, well, let's just say God understands.

God has to understand. If the prophet Jeremiah quotes God accurately, even if you drop the occasional f-bomb in your angry prayers, relax—God does too. God uses the f-word in anger in Jeremiah 3:1–3, where God is chewing out the people of Israel for pleasuring other gods:

> *If a man divorces his wife*
> *and she goes from him*
> *and becomes another man's wife,*
> *will he return to her?*
> *Would not such a land be greatly polluted?*
> *You have played the whore with many lovers;*
> *and would you return to me?*
> *says the Lord,*
> *Look up to the bare heights, and see!*
> *Where have you not been ravished?*
> *By the waysides you have sat waiting for lovers,*
> *like a nomad in the wilderness.*
> *You have polluted the land*
> *with your whoring and wickedness.*
> *Therefore the showers have been withheld,*

and the spring rain has not come;
yet you have the forehead of a whore;
you refuse to be ashamed.

Do you detect God saying the f-word in this English-language version of the passage from Jeremiah? Probably not, but it is there—in the original Hebrew, anyway.

In this extended metaphor, God is emphasizing God's faithfulness to the people of Israel while Israel has been cheating with other nations' gods. God casts Godself as a faithful husband to a woman who has become a prostitute. And not just any kind of prostitute, God says; Israel has become some kind of lusty nympho with no self-control when it comes to other gods to whom she is willing to give herself completely.

In the original Hebrew, the verb that is translated as "ravished" is actually much more coarse. Pronounced *shagal*, the Hebrew verb for "vigorous consensual sex" is noted as *obscene* in the well-respected *Brown-Driver-Briggs Hebrew and English Lexicon* of the Bible. Most Hebrew scholars define *shagal* as the Hebrew verb most like the English f-word. The implication of "Where have you not been *shagalled*?" draws the connection between the land of Israel and the body of a woman: She has wanted to be *shagalled* everywhere a woman can be *shagalled*—if you know what I mean—and most likely for her personal gain.

As a side note, the use of the word *whore* is one example from a list of words that I would never use today, literally or figuratively, but that the Bible thinks is totally okay! While the Bible writers often struggled with using adult words for human body parts, they thought nothing of calling somebody "Whorey Whore McWhore-Whore" at the drop of a hat.

So when it comes to the vocabulary necessary to capture your feelings in your angry prayers, you're probably overthinking things when it comes to profanity and vulgar language. God has heard it all. God can take it. Yet I do have one word of caution. When calling on God to curse another living person or demand that God do harm to the "unrighteous," think twice. Sometimes God does follow through on curses.

If the Bible can be trusted, sometimes calling for God to smite an enemy can work. Such is the famous case of the prophet Elisha, who had just performed the miracle of saving a town's water supply when he was teased by some unruly youths for being, of all things, bald (2 Kings 2:23–24):

> He went up from there to Bethel; and as he was going up on the way, some small boys came out of the city and jeered at him, saying, "Go away, baldhead! Go away, baldhead!" When he turned around and saw them, he cursed them in the name of the Lord. Then two she-bears came out of the woods and mauled forty-two of the boys.

Here's a gang of snotty, smart-aleck teenagers giving this poor good, holy man grief about his male pattern baldness, and next thing they know they're fighting for their lives against rampaging she-bears! That'll teach them—but what do we learn?

The Bible does not record the prophet Elisha's response to the Great She-Bear Massacre. For all we know, Elisha might have been just as surprised as those kids when God answered his angry prayer. He might have said, "Oh, *skubalon*, what have I done now?" and run back into his house and hidden from the cops. But the lesson here is this: As you name and proclaim your pain, be mindful of the power of your words. Say whatever you have to say, express yourself freely, say it as often as you need to in order to feel better, to feel as though God is hearing you exactly the way you want to be heard— but also be ready not to live in that place of anger any longer than you have to. The goal is to let go, not hold on harder to your angry feelings. The final stage and ultimate goal of angry prayer is "reframing," not revenge.

Chapter Eight

PRAYERS OF ANGER, PRAYERS OF TRUTH

While on the surface this chapter may appear to be full of angry prayers, to me it's full of stories. Each prayer represents a person—some of these people I have known well, others just casually; some I just saw on TV talking about their God-anger and I wrote a prayer and sent it to them; many were struggling in their communication with the Divine; some of them were soul sick.

My process was a fairly simple one. Whenever called upon to help somebody pray through their anger, I would take their words, their feelings, their frustrations and "plug them" into an existing lament or curse psalm of the Bible. The result was often eye-opening. Not only did these rewrites breathe new life into some of the obscure language of the psalms, but hearing their problems channeled through the prayers of the Bible seemed to bless their struggles.

"Prayer is so important in Judaism because it is the speech of the soul," says my friend Rabbi Chaim Goldberger. "The soul, in Jewish tradition, is described by the classic commentators as the spirit that speaks."

As a chaplain intern and as a pastor, you meet a lot of spirits who have lost the ability to speak. It is said that every chaplain should be equal parts poet, prophet, and priest. The poet guides the afflicted in finding the words to express their pain while the prophet amplifies the patient's voice as he or she speaks their truth to power. The priestly role blesses the whole process and all the transitions of life. Being with somebody as they begin to pray again puts you in a sacred space.

"Any prayer expresses the sound of the soul speaking," says Rabbi Goldberger, "but angry prayer expresses the sound of the soul holding nothing back, howling from its depths, laying bare its aching yearning and its bitter frustration, its sweeping vision and its crushing disappointment, its terrifying fragility and its instinctive faith. The display of raw religious passion found in angry prayer is truly breathtaking; and breathtaking prayers are the ones that get answered."

I'd like to think that Rabbi Goldberger is right, but perhaps being able to pray again in any form is itself an answer to a prayer.

What follows are seventeen angry prayers that deal with a range of experience from the frustratingly mundane to the cosmically crushing. Just as in the Bible, not all of these prayers end with the "reframing" piece because, at the time these prayers were written, the subject of the prayer may not have been ready to call a truce yet. It is my hope that if I saw them today, their prayer might have a new ending that reframes their pain.

HOW TO PRAY WHEN YOU'RE PISSED AT GOD

AN ANGRY PRAYER FOR RELIEF FROM EVIL PEOPLE

Where the hell are you, O Lord?
Where are you when people like me need you?
The Persistently Evil hunt down the weak
who do not stand a chance against them—
and where are you?
The Persistently Evil brag about how rules don't
    apply to them,
what they can get away with,
and why they never get caught.
They make heroes out of the wicked.
They openly mock you.
And what are you doing about them?
Nothing.

In their pride, the Persistently Evil treat you like
    crap,
yet they are the rich ones!
They've got big houses and really nice clothes,
and I'm broke and don't own anything of value
and drive a piece-of-shit car that always breaks
    down.

The Persistently Evil are self-absorbed
and do not care about anybody but themselves;
they sneer at those they step on.
And what's worse, they say to themselves,
"Nothing will shake me. I know powerful people;
    I'm bullet-proof;
I'll always be happy; I'll never have trouble."
And so far they are right!

Their mouths are full of curses, lies, and threats;
trouble and evil are under their tongue.

I'm not just talking about murderers, drug dealers,
*   rapists, and robbers,*
and others who watch in secret for victims,
but also those people who kill and rob the spirit of
*   the innocent*
in order to profit from their pain.
The Persistently Evil are on the watch for the weak
*   and innocent;*
like predators they know which ones they can
*   exploit.*
They wait like a lion in the grass to catch the
*   helpless and drag them off.*
Then the weak are slowly crushed and they collapse
*   exhausted.*
And after they've satisfied their lust and their
*   gluttony,*
the Persistently Evil say to themselves,
"God has forgotten; God covers his face and never
*   sees it."*

So, get off your ass, Lord!
Lift up your hand, O God.
Do not forget the helpless!
Why do these wicked people revile God?
Why do they say to themselves,
"There is no God; I have nothing to fear!"
Because you aren't doing anything, O God, that's
*   why!*
You see the trouble and grief but
*   you do nothing.*
You don't want blood on your hands, but
*   somehow*
you don't mind the blood flowing from the wounds
*   of the weak and innocent.*
Do something!

HOW TO PRAY WHEN YOU'RE PISSED AT GOD

The victims are crying out to you;
you are the helper of the helpless!

WHY DON'T THE PEOPLE WHO ARE DOING EVIL
    GET CANCER?
Why not give them a brain tumor
so that they might learn that there are
    consequences;
show them what it feels like to be in pain,
to have their head in a vise?
Why aren't large groups of them killed in car
    crashes,
instead of high school kids coming back from
    church camp,
where they spent a summer glorifying your Holy
    Name?

The Lord is Lord forever and ever.
We'll all be gone, but you'll still be here, God.
So if you are listening, O Lord—and I know you
    are—
please heed the cries of the afflicted;
encourage them, listen to their cries
and do something.
Defend the defenseless and the oppressed,
so that we frail humans may be terrified by the
    Wicked no more. Amen.

AN ANGRY PRAYER FOR SOMEBODY
ALONE AT THE HOUR OF DEATH

O Lord, the God who saves me,
day and night I cry out before you.

*May my prayer come before you from this hospital
    bed;*
turn your ear to my cry.

For my soul is full of trouble
and my life draws near the grave.
I am counted among those who will go to hell;
I have no strength.
I am buried alive, set apart with the dead
whom you remember no more,
who are cut off from your care,
with no one to comfort them.
I am scared, and the drugs are no match for my pain.
You have put me in the darkest depths;
my life has always been filled with fear and dread
because of parents who knew only how to drink
and how to hurt and not to love.
I never recovered;
I never learned better.
Your wrath lies heavily upon me now;
*I am overwhelmed with waves of despair and
      loneliness.*

You have taken from me my closest friends
and have made me repulsive to those who still come
    to see me.
I am confined and cannot escape;
my eyes are dim with grief.
I call to you, O Lord, every day;
I spread out my hands to you.
Do you show your wonders to the dead?
Do the dead rise up and praise you?

Is your love declared in the grave,
your faithfulness in Destruction?

HOW TO PRAY WHEN YOU'RE PISSED AT GOD

Are your wonders known in the place of darkness,
or your righteous deeds in the land of oblivion?

But I cry to you for help, O Lord;
in the morning my prayer comes before you.
Why, O Lord, do you reject me
and hide your face from me?
From my youth I have been afflicted and close to
*   death;*
I have suffered your terrors and I am in despair.
Your wrath has swept over me;
your terrors have destroyed me.
All day long they surround me like a flood;
they have completely engulfed me.
You have taken my companions and loved ones
*   from me;*
darkness is my closest friend.

AN ANGRY PRAYER FOR A
VICTIM OF CORPORATE GREED

Hear me, O God, as I voice my complaint;
protect my life from the threat of the greedy.
Hide me from the conspiracy of the powerful,
from that cunning crowd of corporate assholes
who rob even while portraying themselves as hapless
*   victims who should be pitied!*
They sharpen their legal tongues like swords
and aim their words like deadly arrows
at the hardworking, the retired, the powerless.
They ambush the innocent, making empty promises
*   of shared prosperity,*
then shoot their investors and their employees and
*   steal their futures suddenly,*

*without fear of penalty, telling the powerless that it
    couldn't be helped:
the company had to go bankrupt,
the retirement fund had to be raided,
the health insurance had to be canceled.
Blah, blah, blah.*

*The board members and executives encourage each
    other
in their evil schemes,
doling out huge bonuses and enormous
    compensation packages,
while still crying poverty to the world.
They openly connive to lay snares for the unwitting;
they say, "Who will see us?"
They plot injustice and stand up in court
and say, "We were doing it for the shareholders!"
They abscond, leaving others holding an empty bag,
their pockets tearing with the profits they have
    reaped.*

*Will God suddenly strike them down?
No. At least, not enough of them.
Will they not live to enjoy their giant homes and
    pools?
So far.
But wait!
God will turn their own tongues against them,
and they will be consumed by their own greed; until
    they are licking the walls of their own intestines;
all who see them will shake their heads in disgust
    and scorn.*

*Let the righteous rejoice in the Lord and take refuge
    in him;
let all the upright in heart praise him!*

HOW TO PRAY WHEN YOU'RE PISSED AT GOD

AN ANGRY PRAYER FOR A
WOMAN LONGING FOR A FAMILY

You showed favor to my parents, O Lord;
you restored their fortunes after setbacks and
tragedies.
You forgave the infidelity of my grandfathers
and covered all the sins of my ancestors.
You set aside all your wrath and turned from your
fierce anger,
allowing them to flourish and enjoy long lives
and marriages and many adoring generations.

I am a sinner;
I have regrets about giving my body to men who did
not love me.
I have ravaged this body with chemicals,
preventing it from conceiving life,
choosing instead to live life on my own terms.

O God, do not be silent; listen to your servant once
more.
Do not let freedom be my curse!
Restore my health now, O God our Savior,
and put away your displeasure toward me.
Will you be angry with me forever?
Will you prolong your anger by denying me future
generations?
Are my sins worse than my father's?

Have I not always been honest and giving?
Why do you curse me?
Why am I not deserving of love?
If the beasts of the forest can find companionship,
then why not me?
Have I not been a good daughter, a good friend?

Will you not revive me again?
Direct toward me someone who could love me,
and me toward him,
so that together we might raise a child in your
honor!

I will listen to what God the Lord will say;
God promises peace to his people, God's saints,
as long as they do not return to the foolishness of
their youth.
Some return to their sins—drugs, child abuse, sex,
neglect—
yet they are blessed with children over and over
while I live alone with only my animals to care for
me!
But can an animal say my name with love
and place his little hand on my face?

Love and faithfulness meet together;
righteousness and peace kiss each other.
Faithfulness springs forth from the earth,
and righteousness looks down from heaven.
The Lord will indeed give me what is good,
and my body will yield its harvest.
Righteousness goes before God and prepares the
way for my steps.

An Angry Prayer for a Victim of Bullying by More Popular Kids

Listen up, God, as I voice my complaint;
protect me from the tyranny of the popular,
from the morality of the cool.
Hide me from the conspiracy of the insecure,

HOW TO PRAY WHEN YOU'RE PISSED AT GOD

*from the kids who cover over their failings by
     exploiting others.
I do not feel attractive, I may not be athletic,
but you are my God.
You know how I am disgraced and shamed;
all my enemies are before you.*

*Humiliation has broken me,
and I am vulnerable to attack from all sides;
I looked for sympathy, but there was none;
for comforters, but I found none.
I cried out for you during ridicule after ridicule, O
     God,
but you were silent.*

*The tyrannical cool spit in my food,
and after gym class they gave me urine for my thirst.
They tripped me and stripped me
and made me look foolish in the locker room.
They called me names to my face
without fear of consequence, for I am weak.
I fight back with witticisms,
but they are impervious to my stinging barbs.
They sit at the coveted cafeteria tables like kings and
     queens
while I eat in fear.*

*O God! May their eyes be dimmed
so that they would need thick glasses too;
may glossy, bouncy hair grow only on their backs;
may they lose their beautiful posture
and walk bent over, forever staring at their shoes,
feeling shame every day as they walk past the
     popular.
May their yearbook picture be the last great photo
     of them!*

Pour out your wrath on them for what they have
      done to the blemished.
May the tyrannical cool graduate to toil at jobs
where they are undervalued;
may they feel your desertion always.
Let them understand what it's like to fear what
      somebody has done
to their food and drink.
For they persecute the geeky and the awkward.

Charge them, God, with crime upon crime;
do not let them share in your salvation.
May they be blotted out of the book of life
and not be listed among the righteous.
I am in pain and distress;
may your salvation, O God, protect me.

I will praise God's name in song
and glorify God with thanksgiving.
This will please the Lord more than those
whose pledge of allegiance is only lip service at the
      flagpole.
The meek will see and be glad;
those who seek God, may your hearts live!
The Lord hears the pleas of the nerdy
and does not despise those held captive by bad skin,
      teeth, and hair.

Let heaven and earth praise God,
for God will save the uncool in their math clubs
and rebuild their broken spirits;
their children will be many,
and someday they will finally know love and
      acceptance. Amen.

HOW TO PRAY WHEN YOU'RE PISSED AT GOD

AN ANGRY PRAYER FOR SOMEBODY SUFFERING WITH DEPRESSION DURING THE HOLIDAYS

As a dog pants for a bowl of water,
so my soul thirsts for you, O God.
My soul thirsts for any sign of God,
for a living, not historical, God.
But I'm still like a dog because you do not feed,
and I only get by on what I am eating from my lawn.
Is there someplace where God will meet me
*   halfway?*
My tears have been my food day and night,
while people say to me, "Where is your God?
If you believe, why won't your God heal you?
If you are not healed then maybe God does not
*   believe in you!"*

These things I remember as I pour out my soul:
I used to go to church;
I sang in the choir in the house of God,
with shouts of joy and thanksgiving among the
*   festive throng.*
And then depression gripped me,
and now my house of worship
might as well be a house of pancakes.

The joy of the holidays became my enemy,
and holiday decorations mocked my soul.
I am haunted by the difference between what I once
*   had*
and the way I live now.
Where shall you go, O my soul, until the New Year?
Why are you so disturbed within me?
I yell at myself, "Put your hope in God!
Remember when God did great things for you!"

*I once heard God calling me from the roar of
     waterfalls;*
waves and breakers swept over me once.
*Now I can no longer hear God through the fog of
     my depression.*
I say to God, "Why have you forgotten me?
Will you ever break me free of this?"

But you are God and I am not.
I fear I am nothing.

AN ANGRY PRAYER FOR THE
POOR WITH CAR TROUBLE

God, save me; O Lord, come quickly.
My transportation is as poor and needy as I am.
When it breaks down, I break down;
no one seems willing to help.
"Take the bus," the heartless say,
as if a bus will magically appear when I need it
and take me where I need to go.
*"Buy a better car," the callous say, as if I had the
     money!*
If I had any money I would fix this one!
And so here I sit again on the side of the road,
     fearful, already late for life,
knowing that my downward spiral will continue
and no one will help me.

May those who look down their nose on me
*but do nothing to help be put to shame and
     confusion;*
*may their engines blow up the day after their
     warranties run out.*

HOW TO PRAY WHEN YOU'RE PISSED AT GOD

May those who say to me, "Hey, serves you right for
*   all your bad life decisions,*
for all the mistakes you've made,"
discover tears in their own safety nets.
For I am poor and screwed up, O God, and only to
*   you do I submit for judgment,*
and only you can give me justice.
I do not turn to you to make me rich;
I only beg you, Don't punish me for being as broke
*   as my car!*

May all who seek you rejoice and be glad in you.
But please don't restrict your grace to people who
*   are already rich.*
I am poor and love you; come quickly to me;
O Lord, do not delay, for I am late again,
my boss hates me enough already,
and I am beyond desperate. Amen.

An Angry Prayer of Lonely Desperation

Hey you, O Lord? Remember me?
The person who has always been committed to you?
How long will you hide your face from me?
How long must I struggle with my darkest doubts
without the comfort of your voice?
I feel you have abandoned me!
Has this been a one-way relationship all along?
When will it be my turn to succeed and thrive?
Is this fun for you?

Look me in the eye and answer me, O Lord my
*   God.*
Either give me light or I will just die in the dark.

If I go down, those people who take pleasure
in the ruin of my life will say, "I win."
They will laugh and rejoice.
Is that what you want?
Remember, I've always been on your side, God!

I trust in your love; my heart rejoices in your
salvation.
I will sing to the Lord, for God has been good to me.
Even if right now all I can think of is how shitty
things are.
Amen.

An Angry Prayer for Personal Justice

To you I call, O Lord my Rock, but you remain
silent.
I am in hell.
I need your mercy; I call to you for help,
because I am guilty over my rage.
I lift up my hands to your Most Holy Place.

Don't punish me along with the Persistently Evil,
those who speak cordially with their family and
friends
but harbor really sick secrets in their hearts;
those who like to stir up trouble whenever and
wherever they can
because their souls are in such turmoil
that they hate to see others living in peace.

Why don't you mess up their lives for a while?
Why don't you repay them for what their hands
have done

*and bring down upon them the bad karma they
        deserve
instead of throwing more crap at me than I can
        possibly handle right now?
Since they show no regard for the works of the Lord
and don't believe you exist,
why not show them how wrong they are;
make them an example of what happens to those
        who don't believe in you—
instead of screwing with those who love and
        worship you?*

*Then I will proclaim, "Look what God's hands have
        done!
God will tear them down and never build them up
        again!
Serves them right!"*

*Praise be to the Lord, for God has heard my cry for
        mercy.
The Lord is my strength, and God is like a search
        engine;
he knows all, and I am helped.
My heart leaps for joy and I will give thanks to God
        in song.*

*The Lord is the strength of his people,
a fortress of salvation for his anointed.
Save your people and bless your inheritance;
be their shepherd and carry them forever. Amen.*

An Angry Prayer for a Victim of Lies

Vindicate me, O God, and plead my cause
against those who are spreading rumors about me;
rescue me from the deceitful and the wicked
who are strangling me with their lies.
I cry to you that I might be understood;
I ask you to bridge the gap between who you know
    I am
and what people say about me.
Please bring me home.

Those who were once my friends are content to
    make me miserable,
and you, O God, seem content to let this happen!
You are God, my stronghold. Will you reject me
    too?
Must I endure this oppression alone?

Send forth your light and your truth;
let them guide me;
let them bring me to your holy mountain,
to the place where you dwell,
so that I may feel that somebody understands me.
Tell me the words to say
to cut through the walls of lies that are imprisoning
    me.
Then will I go to the altar of God,
to God, my joy and my delight.
I will praise you with music,
O God, my God.

I tell my lonely soul, put your hope in the light and
    truth of the Lord!
For I will yet praise him, my Savior and my God.
    Amen.

AN ANGRY PRAYER FOR A DYING CONGREGATION, THE VICTIM OF VANDALISM

Why have you rejected us, O God?
Why does your anger smolder against the sheep of
    your pasture?
Remember the people you purchased of old,
this congregation of your inheritance, whom you
    redeemed,
this house of worship where you once dwelt?

Once our pews were full and our services were
    many.
Our sermons were on the lips of the righteous;
the Sunday schools were full of happy, noisy
    children.
The walls were painted, the parking lot was paved
    and smooth,
and there was money enough to help others.
But now look at this place.
Turn your steps toward these everlasting ruins;
see all the destruction that apathy has brought upon
    your sanctuary.
No one fears us for they do not fear you.

Now the enemies of God roar
in the places where you once met with us.
Kids break in and use cans of spray paint
to set up their colors as signs against you.
They have behaved like men wielding axes
to cut through a thicket of trees.
They have smashed all the carved paneling.
They have burned your sanctuary;
they have defiled the dwelling place of your
    Name.

*They have said in their hearts, "We will crush them
    completely!"*
*They seek to burn every place where God is
    worshipped in the land.*

*We are given no miraculous signs; no prophets are
    left,*
*and none of us knows how long this will continue to
    go on.*
How long will the enemy mock you, O God?
*Will those who worship at the cash register, the sale
    rack,*
*and at sporting events on the Sabbath revile your
    name forever?*
Why do you hold back your right hand?
*Take it from the folds of your garment and destroy
    those things!*

But you, O God, are my King from of old;
you bring salvation upon the earth.
It was you who split open the sea by your power;
*you who killed off the dinosaurs in the waters and
    on the land*
and gave humans dominion over the earth.
It was you who crushed the heads of monsters
and gave food to the creatures of the desert.
It was you who opened up springs and streams;
*you dried up the ever flowing rivers and gave us
    land to farm.*
The day is yours, and yours also the night;
you established the sun and moon.
It was you who set all the boundaries of the earth;
you made both summer and winter.

*Remember how the enemy has mocked you, O
    Lord,*

how foolish people revile your Name.
Do not hand over the life of your dove to wild
    beasts;
do not forget the lives of your afflicted people
    forever.

Have regard for your covenant,
for the dark places of the land are full of the haunts
    of violence.
Do not let the oppressed retreat in disgrace;
may the poor and needy praise your name.
Rise up, O God, and defend your cause;
remember how fools mock you all day long
using baseball bats and graffiti.
Do not ignore the clamor of your adversaries,
the uproar of your enemies.
Save this poor church
as we have tried to save people for you! Amen.

AN ANGRY PRAYER FOR THE ABUSERS OF CHILDREN

O Lord, the God who avenges, shine forth.
Rise up, O Judge of the earth;
avenge those who hurt children, your children;
hurt the abusers with just punishment.
How can you allow this?
How long, O Lord, will the Persistent Evil Ones,
be allowed to slap, punch, kick, burn, stab, shoot,
rape, and murder the children in their care?
They pour out their violent punishments,
full of boasting that their victims will not be
    believed,
fearing no consequences from you—you who see all.

They crush the most vulnerable of your people,
    O Lord;
they sexually enslave babies!
And still you do not strike them down!
The Persistently Evil are reckless and cause
    "accidents";
they imperil the meekest,
even the child whom they are paid to take into their
    homes;
they raise messed up children who crave power and
    attention,
who act out their pain on others so that the cycle
    continues for generations.
They say, "The Lord does not see; the God of justice
    pays no attention."

Take heed, you mothers without mercy, you fathers
    without fear!
Does the one who planted the ear in babies not hear?
Does the one who formed the infant's eye not see?
Does the one who disciplines nations not punish?
Does the one who wrote the first laws lack
    knowledge?
Blessed is the disciplined parent, O Lord,
who controls his hand and curbs her tongue.
Bless the good with an extra portion,
but dig a pit by the side of the road for the bodies of
    the wicked!

For the Lord will not reject his people.
Judgment will again be founded on righteousness,
and all the upright in heart will follow it.

Who will rise up for me against the wicked?
Who will take a stand for me against the evil?

When the child says, "My foot is slipping,"
may your love, O Lord, support him.
When anxiety is great within her,
may your consolation bring joy to her soul.
Can corrupt parents be allied with you—
those who bring on misery at every turn?
The Persistently Evil know how to hide in the
    throngs;
they band together with the righteous in public
but condemn the innocent to death in secret.
But the Lord has become my fortress,
let it be a defense for the innocents.
God will repay the Persistently Evil for their sins
and destroy them for their wickedness;
the Lord our God will rot them from the inside out.
    Amen.

AN ANGRY PRAYER FOR SOMEBODY FIGHTING A TERMINAL ILLNESS

In you, O Lord, I have taken refuge
from this disease that consumes my body;
deliver me from this pain and all these indignities;
be my refuge, a strong fortress around me as my
    muscles fail.

I cannot control my bodily functions anymore;
I feel so vulnerable.
Lead and guide me.
Help me to allow others to tend to me.

My heart is filled with resentment at
those who worship money or sex or power
but enjoy perfect health.

I trust in the Lord.
Why am I plunged into the depths of this shit?
I know you have seen my affliction, O Lord,
and you know the anguish of my soul.
You have not handed me over to death
You have set me in a warm place to heal.

Be merciful to me, for I am hurting;
my eyes grow weak with sorrow,
my soul and my body are wasted with grief.

My co-workers are afraid of saying something
    wrong
so they say nothing at all;
I am a horror to my friends;
those who see me on the street flee from me
because they fear the answer to the question
"How are you doing?"
I am forgotten, as if I were dead, but I am standing
    right here!
I have become like a hard drive in a broken
    computer—
I have all this stored knowledge but no one will
    access it because
it's too much trouble; it's easier to pull the plug, get
    a new friend, and start over.

But I trust in you, O Lord;
I say, "You are my Friend!"
Shine on me, console me when my friends let me
    down;
keep me safe from negligent tongues.

Praise be to the Lord,
for God has shown wonderful love in the past.

*In my alarm I said, "Hey, it's me over here in the
    sick bed!"*
*You heard me cry when I called for help? You have
    heard me call out?*

*Love the Lord, all the saints! The Lord preserves the
    faithful;*
But he pays back the proud.
*Be strong and take heart, all you who hope in the
    Lord.*
I hope.

AN ANGRY PRAYER FOR THOSE WHO ARE CUT OFF IN TRAFFIC

O God, whom I praise, do not remain silent.
*Wicked and deceitful people have screwed me and
    used me, your servant;*
they have humiliated me for the last time.
With big, fast SUVs and aggressive attitudes
they surround me like eels;
they attack me without cause.
*In return for my selflessness they cut me off in
    traffic.*
Don't they see my bumper sticker?
I am a person of prayer.
I abide by the law.
I stay in my lane and in my peace.
I just want to be left alone.

The evil drivers repay my good with evil,
my courtesy with ugliness.
*They act like you, O Lord, made the roads just for
    them;*

they treat me like a slave.
They make evil faces and hand gestures and yell
*   hurtful words*
even when they pass me at my expense!

Plague them, O God;
put a bigger abuser in their path.
When they try to pass, let them be run off the road.
May their remaining days be few;
may their children be orphans and their spouses die
*   alone without health care.*
May their families be driven from their homes,
ruined by black mold that cannot be eradicated.
May a creditor seize all they have;
may strangers lay hands on all their good stuff.
May no one extend kindness to them or take pity on
*   their children.*

May their descendants be cut off,
their names blotted out from the next generation.
May the iniquity of a father be remembered before
*   the Lord;*
may the sin of a mother never be blotted out.
As they have cut me off, may their memory be wiped
*   out from the earth.*

For those who hound the timid never think of doing
*   a kindness;*
they only torment to death the weak and those with
*   shattered nerves,*
racing their powerful engines and sounding their
*   sharp horns.*
The last guy who refused to let me merge
pronounced a curse on me with his lips and his
*   finger:*

may his meanness come back on him;
may your blessing be far from him in his time of
    need.
May the curse of his finger enter into his own body
    in the most painful place.
May the evil sink into his bones like oil.
May his arrogant selfishness be like a scarf wrapped
    around his neck;
like the twisted metal of a wreck, may it envelop
    him forever.

May this be the Lord's payment to my abusers,
to those who do evil to me.
But you, O Sovereign Lord, be fair to me.
For I am sick and tired, and my heart is wounded.
I am fading away like an evening shadow;
I am shaken off like a locust.
I am an object of scorn to other drivers;
when they see me, they shake their heads.

Help me, O Lord my God;
save me in accordance with your love.
Let them know that it is your hand,
that you, O Lord, have done it.
They may curse me as they will,
but when they attack they will be put to shame.
And I, your servant, will rejoice.
For God will snap me from the jaws of death,
even as they will only find my abuser's body with
    the Jaws of Life.

AN ANGRY PRAYER FOR THE VICTIMS OF TERRORISM

I see it on the History Channel, O God;
our parents have told us what you did for them
back in the day, in days long ago.
With your hand you drove out
the Hitlers and the Stalins;
you kept human hearts hopeful
through the terrors of dictators and would-be
    conquerors;
you planted our ancestors in new lands
and made them flourish.
Not by their hands did they win World War II,
nor did their arms bring them victory;
it was your *right hand,* your *arm, and the light of*
    your *face,*
for you loved other generations before us—
you have loved other generations more than us.

Through you we try to push back those who seek
    our destruction
and those who spread pain around the world.

But now you have rejected and humbled us;
you no longer go out with our armies;
we are alone.
You made us retreat before the enemy
and allowed terrorists to kill our boys and girls
who had so much promise and loved you their whole
    lives.
Murderers have wrapped themselves in bombs made
    in your name.
Bombs made in your name have plundered us
and stolen our most precious treasures—our
    children, our hope.

HOW TO PRAY WHEN YOU'RE PISSED AT GOD

You have given us up to be devoured like sheep
and have scattered us among the nations.

All this happened to us, though we had not
    forgotten you,
nor had we broken your commandments.
Our hearts had not turned back;
our feet had not strayed from your path.
But you have crushed us, made us easy prey for
    terrorists,
and covered us with deep darkness.
If we had forgotten the name of our God
or stretched out our hands to a foreign god,
would not you have discovered it,
since God knows the secrets of the heart?

Awake, O Lord! Why do you sleep? Rouse yourself!
Do not reject us forever.
Why do you hide your face and forget our misery
    and oppression?
Roadside bombs have brought us down to the dust;
our bodies are flung to the ground
and lie in the wreckage of our aircraft sent to bring
    aid!
Rise up and help us; restore our respect;
lead us once more and show us how to be a force for
    good. Amen.

AN ANGRY PRAYER OF SOMEBODY LOSING THEIR NEIGHBORHOOD TO CRIME

Listen to my prayer, O God;
do not ignore my cries;
hear me and answer me!

My thoughts trouble me and I am distraught
at the proud voices of the street gangs,
their smug, wicked stares at the news cameras;
for they bring down suffering upon their own
*   people,*
their own family and friends,
and fill us with fear of retribution if we stand up to
*   them.*

My heart is in anguish;
the terrors of death assail me.
Fear and trembling own me;
horror has overwhelmed me.
I said, "O, that I had the wings of a dove!
I would fly away and be at rest;
I would flee far away and live in a safe
*   neighborhood,*
just a small house.
I would hurry to my place of shelter,
far from the bullets and bullying."

Confuse the gangbangers, O Lord;
still their tongues;
stop them from recruiting our babies to be their foot
*   soldiers.*
For there is violence and pain in my city.
Day and night they prowl about its walls like
*   vermin;*
malice and abuse drive slowly through our
*   neighborhoods,*
with loud stereos pounding;
and the police are no match.

If it were an enemy insulting me, I could endure it;
if a gangbanger were raising himself against me, I
*   could hide.*

But when somebody you love—
a friend, a family member, a neighbor child,
somebody with whom you once enjoyed sweet
    fellowship in the house of God—
becomes part of that evil, I cannot bear it.
O Lord, help us;
shield the children who have yet to be corrupted.
Stop the gangs who are killing our children
and taking our neighborhoods down with them.

Let death take these gangs by surprise, sudden and
    painful;
let them go down alive to the grave, kicking and
    screaming,
for evil finds lodging among them;
let death take these gangs in the public square
so that truth can be restored,
the goodness of the world is reordered, and
children everywhere will no longer be prey
to those who make the ways of evil seem blessed.

The devil's speech is smooth as ice cream from a
    musical truck,
yet war is in his heart;
the devil's words are soothing like warm hand lotion,
yet they produce bloodshed, drug addiction, and
    fatherless babies,
actions without consequences, cities without hope.

Cast your cares on the Lord and God will sustain
    you!
God will never let the righteous fall.
But you, O God, will bring down the wicked into
    the pit of corruption;
bloodthirsty and deceitful men should not live out
    half their days.

Save them or kill them, Lord, but
do not let them thrive. Amen.

AN ANGRY PRAYER AGAINST
CAMPAIGN COMMERCIALS

Hey, you so-called servants of the people!
Are you doing God's work?
No, your hearts drip with injustice,
your hands mete out violence on the earth,
and you hide your self-serving deeds behind slick
     TV packaging!

Since you were babies you've been crying,
mostly about yourselves;
from the womb you have learned to say anything to
     get ahead.
Your words are like the venom of a viper;
you seek to mesmerize the people
like a charmer hypnotizing by playing his pipe.

Break their white, shining teeth in their mouths,
     O God,
that they may be nourished only on the kibble of
     their discontent!
O Lord, let the deceitful dry up like the tax money
     they drain away for their own purposes;
when they hold up the taxpayers at gunpoint,
please see to it that they shoot themselves in the ass.
Like a slug on a hot sidewalk that melts as it moves
     along,
may their efforts lead to nothing but their own
     demise.
Then the disbelieving will finally say, "Oh, I guess
     there is a God after all." Amen.

Chapter Nine

CONCLUSION

At the beginning of this book, I made some promises about reconsidering the value of appropriate, righteous anger; rediscovering the role of prayer in releasing anger; and why learning to process anger through prayer— especially anger at God—positively affects our emotional, spiritual, mental, and physical health. I emphasized how important it is to pray truthfully even if those angry prayers are ugly sounding or seemingly blasphemous.

I hope I have made the comforting point that there is no shame in angry prayer, that gut-wrenching honesty in our prayers can be therapeutic, and that God is not as hung up on our human vocabulary as we are. Praying when you're pissed at the world, at others, and/or at God can follow the classic, three-part biblical structure of "name, proclaim, reframe" or you can go freestyle and just riff away. Just let out what you're feeling. There is no wrong way of praying through your anger except to not pray at all.

I have strived to make my case a blend of scientific, psychological, and biblical testimony on the validity of

God-focused angry prayer. We learned that whenever we humans—not just people of faith but even agnostics and atheists—*contemplate* God, we "enhance the neural functioning of the brain in ways that improve physical and emotional health," according to the research of Dr. Andrew Newberg.

The only hitch? Regardless of whether we're angry about other humans or about God, when we are angry for a prolonged period of time, our neural processes and our bodies begin to perform badly. So we have to be mindful of the things that are making us angry at the world, other people, and/or God and try to deal with those emotions as fast as possible. Angry prayer can assist us in doing this. Let's face it, we are never truly healthy until we are at our peak—in mind, body, and soul. And anger is one thing that depletes all parts of who we are in drastic and sometimes frightening ways.

Moreover, this book has attempted to recognize the complexity of the problem of maddening frustration, pain, and hard feelings and the simplicity of the solution: Name your pain, proclaim your pain, and reframe your pain, even if the process takes a while.

Dr. Judith Orloff concludes, "Many people can't let go of anger because their egos are involved and they are more interested in being right. As a psychiatrist I've seen every variation of anger. It can be healthy and unhealthy. Anger is a human emotion and most of the time it controls people rather than people taming it."

For some people, sometimes taming that anger requires more than what I offer in this book. There is no shame in therapy, psychiatry, and necessary medication because every human brain is like a computer that is made up of both software and hardware. The software is our consciousness and our psyche, that is, the "life programs" we use to guide us, and they are influenced by our birth families, experiences, parental involvement, education, peers, and so forth. The physical brain's hardware includes our biochemical balance, neural pathways, genes, and so on. For those people whose anger defines their life, I hope I have started a useful conversation. Psychotherapy and spiritual renewal should never be thought of as mutually exclusive pursuits.

"We need to try and figure out the ways to get the belief systems to turn around and to try to look at something in a more positive way," Newberg told me. "There are a lot of individuals these days who are trying to find ways to integrate what we know about religious and spiritual beliefs with psychotherapy to help people deal with not only their psychological problems but the spiritual elements of those problems as well and to hope to give them a sense of meaning, a sense of purpose and something that can be of value to them that will help get them through that process and past that anger and convert that into something that is more positive and beneficial for them."

Is getting comfortable with angry prayer the key to converting our negative emotions and psychological roadblocks into something more positive and beneficial? As director of the Center for Spirituality and the Mind and the Center for the Integrated Study of Spirituality and the Neurosciences at the University of Pennsylvania, Newberg will be experimenting with the concepts in this book in the future to see how they can help certain patients. He also told me that there should be a study to determine the before-and-after effects of therapeutic angry prayer on the brain. I look forward to seeing if clinical results will match the anecdotal experience and the biblical evidence that suggests that God blesses our anger as long as we're using our prayer as a way to work through it.

Finally, a note about "self-anger." The notion of "kicking oneself" for past deeds is familiar to all of us, but some people do this more than others. Personally, I don't carry around any significant anger toward others or toward God, but I am inclined to judge myself very harshly and withhold self-forgiveness too long. Perhaps you can relate to that. If you are plagued by self-anger, could you write an angry prayer about yourself just to get it out of your system? I mean, really let yourself have it in a prayer to God about all the wrong things you've done—and then start putting all that behind you?

In closing, I want to stress to you the importance that you should include yourself on your list of people you will release from anger, and I want to remind you that heaven is filled with people who are forgiven but hell is full of people who cannot forgive themselves.

Remember, when you write your prayers, you write your story.

When you tell God your story, you tell God your truth.

Remember, if you aren't saying something, you aren't saying anything.

And God *is* listening.

A SELECTION OF ANGRY PRAYERS
FROM EVERYDAY FOLKS

For a time, I had a website where people could write out their anger, frustrations, and prayers. What follows are those prayers and the prayers of some parishioners, co-workers, and friends.

Each one tells a little story. There is a beginning, a middle, and an end. I find each one fascinating, both in light of the theme of the angry prayer and simply in terms of the raw emotion it expresses. What really grips me for the purposes of this book is that each prayer parallels the biblical model for an angry prayer. I have prayed for each one of these people, but I have no idea whether things improved; I know only that they expressed their gratitude for having a place to be heard.

An Angry Prayer from a Former Pastor

Dear God:

I believed in you and served you for so many years. I was a preacher, for crying out loud. Yet you know what? For years, and years, and now decades, I have cried out to you, supplicated you day and night, for one thing, the ONE damn thing, the ONLY thing I want in my life: Love.

I am so lonely that the only thing keeping me from suicide is the fear of the horrible hell that you created for the people you supposedly "love." But you have denied me over and over. You have created absurd, unnatural, unbelievable situations where I am hurt and rejected and lonely. You cannot, I repeat, cannot possibly "love" me when you deny me all human love. Sorry, but you make it really hard to believe in a kind, loving God because of the way that you deny me love. God is love? Sorry, but that is a little hard to believe when you obviously hate love so much.

Sincerely,
Your Fatalist Creation

The Angry Prayer of an Addict and a Black Sheep

Dear God:

I was diseased as a small child. By the time I left home, I was suicidal, chronically depressed, friendless, and an angry alcoholic. God, You know I have never stopped trying.

Although I have made many plans, I have never attempted suicide because I'm afraid that the suffering in this life will be worse in the next. But God, there has never been a day that I wouldn't have preferred to be dead.

I took pills for the depression, and now I'm addicted to the Effexor. I struggle with the side effects, and I worry about what is happening to my brain. I'm still depressed.

I stopped drinking only to find that I need to be addicted to hide the pain. I have never tried hard drugs, and I'm not addicted to gambling. (Thank you for that.) But I can be addicted to anything: work, shopping, food, running, computer solitaire . . . I have overcome addiction after addiction, but the pain never leaves.

I have had an endless string of bad relationships. To my great shame, I was promiscuous at an early age (looking for the love I never had). I don't know how to love.

I have never had a friend, only acquaintances. I don't know what it means to be a friend.

I have tried therapist after therapist, treatment after treatment, and the pain remains. I'm afraid nothing will fix me.

I am the black sheep of my family. The diseased one. The bad daughter. The unwelcome one. The whipping boy. Because of my family, I am diseased. Because of my disease, my family shuns me.

God, You made me strong, and I have survived. But I am so tired.

Please help me to stop dwelling on the past and look toward the future.

Please help me to forgive.

Please show me what I need to change, and help me to learn.

Please teach me to love and to be a good friend so that I can attract these things into my life.

Please help me to get along with others at work, to be more humble, and to enjoy being part of a team.

Please help me to be less self-centered so that I can help others and do Your will.

God, please replace the pain, the regret, the loss, and the anger with forgiveness, tolerance, happiness, and love.

Please take away the fear and leave me with faith. Amen.

*An Angry Prayer from Somebody
Who Feels Marred by God*

God?

I'm confused. Please help me understand. Growing up I realized the pious, self-aggrandizing, money-mongering, blasphemous, egocentric ways people have engaged in religions in your name. I rose above it and gave my heart and soul to you. I devoted my life to you and have strived in every moment to grow closer to you and all your glory. But something puzzles me. . . .

It seems that the closer I get to you, the higher on the ladder I climb, the more I am kicked to the curb like a dog. Why is it that it seems that the assholes of this world can lie, cheat, deceive, steal, rape, pillage, and kill and come out smelling like a rose, but when I just turn my head I'm blasted to my knees by another melee of misfortune? Why is it that good things only seem to happen to bad people, and the salt of the earth gets sand packed up their ass? Uh?

Sometimes I really wonder if you even exist. Sometimes I think that the earth is hell, run by Satan, and the only way we're going to survive is by the law of the jungle . . . "eat or be eaten." Where will it all end? What is it you're trying to prove with me? They say you will never give a person more than he can handle. What do you want? Just what in the hell do you want?

Please give me a break and give someone else a turn at your Divine intervention because I think it sucks. I guess you don't believe you can get more bears with honey than vinegar, uh?

Nope, I didn't think so.

An Angry Prayer for the Bewildered but Hopeful

Dear God,

I've been trained to know you since I was a small child, but I'm still wondering who you are and why you are so quiet.

I've begged you for help with my personal demons but they still stand strong.

I've asked to feel your love and power but only feel empty and powerless.

I've asked you to help me change my life but receive no offerings of help.

I've asked you to help grow my faith in you but the more I ask the less faith I gain.

I've asked you to show me a sign, a glimpse, a hope, and you never show me.

I've asked you for success but failure is all I receive.

I've asked you to change the world, but it remains cruel and Godless.

I'll keep asking you for help, and I'm expecting more silence, . . . but I know I must keep asking because you are God and your will be done not mine.

Angry Prayer for Holiday Cheer

In this season of miracles, the only miracle there is for me is that I am still alive, that I haven't offed myself already.

As my dog pants for a bowl of cool water, my loyal soul pants for you, God. When can I go and meet with God? Is there a toy store window where you're hanging . out with the true joy of the season? Is there a nativity scene on a church lawn? Charlie Brown's humble tree? The Great Pumpkin Patch? The North Pole?

Is there someplace where God will meet me halfway? I'll spend all my money to get there. God just has to show up for a minute—for a second—and tell me that everything is worth fighting for.

As the Bible says, my tears have been my food day and night, while people in the office say, "Christmas is a secular holiday—be happy with that. If you believe, then won't God cure you of this sadness? If you are not healed, then doesn't that prove that there is no God and move on?"

But I cannot "move on" because of what I had once.

These things I remember: I used to go to church. I sang in the choir in the house of God, with shouts of joy and thanksgiving among the festive throng as it says in the brochure. Scripture meant something; sermons actually lifted me up.

And then I grew up. I got dumped a few times right around the holidays. Engagements under the tree that I had prayed for only turned into more dumpings on New Year's Eve.

Since then, depression has gripped me, and my local house of worship might as well be a house of pancakes.

The holidays are now my enemy, an unwelcome visitor that won't leave. The cheerier the holiday decorations, the more I feel mocked.

Why am I so depressed? No husband, no children, no life, only work. My soul is so depressed, Prozac can't reach it within me. God is only a vision from memory.

Once I thought I heard God calling me from the roar of a waterfall. I thought I actually heard God use my name. I went into the cool waters as the white froth swept over me. The waterfall made it misty, and the water droplets stung my eyes. I thought I saw a shadow of God moving through the mist. I thought I heard my name. I knew that God was in that waterfall. My soul thirsts for those waters again.

Now I can no longer hear God through the fog of my depression.

Merry Christmas, my ass.

An Angry Prayer from a Weekend Soul

God, it's me "J." Do you remember me?

I know I pester you constantly, but can you show me why it has to be me?

You have saved my butt many times, but why did you have to put me there to begin with to save?

I always believed in you, always prayed to you, and I have always trusted in you, so why did and does it have to be me? Is it because I said I would believe and be there for you?

But that's what you asked me to do, so how come all the evil stuff had to happen to me?

Growing up on the streets, running from the gangs, can't go home, safer running and sleeping on the streets. What did you want me to learn? Mothers, fathers, and relatives beating, raping, abusing, berating, letting them sell me for child porn, every day making me run, and live in the trees.

So, God, what did I need to learn, and how come it took so long to learn it before you let me grow up and get out of hiding? I have done your work all my life, helping victims, taking care of the elderly, paying everyone's way when they had nothing.

What did I get in return?

Physical decimation, everything I ever get taken away from me as soon as I get it, evil people trying to kill me, rape me, or use me as their tool.

My heart is broken. No one here loves me. Everyone here has hurt me and used me. Was I just your tool to use and toss away as well?

Going to war, digging babies out of bombed buildings, saving women and children from abuse and starvation.

Haven't I done enough yet?

All I want is for the bills to be paid, to get out of the cold, and to be safe. How come I don't get to have that now after a lifetime of doing your work?

An Angry Prayer from a Woman Who Has to Start Again

Dear Lord, thank you for showing me a new path. I didn't choose this path, but I have to trust that your wisdom is greater than what I might think I want.

That husband who I was losing myself in trying to keep him happy? He has left me for another woman. And it isn't about the sex—he even says our sex life was great, fantastic even. But she "makes him feel alive" and "saved his life by pulling him back from the brink." Yes, I am angry—I now have to worry about having contracted a sexually transmitted disease because of his selfishness. Fidelity was everything to him at one point; how could he change so quickly? God, you honestly didn't give me any warning!

I am angry with you, God, because I played by all of the rules and look where it got me! Brokenhearted, fighting for survival every day. But I will not let this crush me. It will make me stronger. I am no longer cutting little pieces of myself off to make my husband happy. I can be honest about my wants, needs, and desires. I can form my own opinions and express them. While I didn't deserve this situation, I am finding out that I am made of stronger stuff than I ever knew.

God, I was so wrong about my parents and my siblings. They have rallied around me, my greatest supporters. Yet I am still angry because it shouldn't have taken a health scare and the end of my marriage to help them realize that I need them.

God, I am angry about what is happening to my children. They are so worried about me and hate their dad right now. Bitterness is something I fight against every day—I don't want this anger and bitterness to take over their hearts. My son is so confused, wanting to be supportive of his dad and then seeing how his dad is treating me; it's tearing him up inside. My other daughter is angry, but is going through the motions. Just like I did to keep her dad happy. I am angry that I modeled this behavior for her.

How can this be happening? I played by all of the rules, was a dutiful, loving wife, mother, etc. So many truths I have believed in have been shattered. God, I feel like if I stop and really think about all of this, I will sink into quicksand. Hopeless that things will ever get better.

An Angry Prayer from a Mourning Widow

A year ago, as you know, my husband died. We had been together for twenty-four years. We even started finishing each other's sentences. You were always there! So what happened? You took him from me, and I haven't heard from you since! I try talking to you, but not a peep from you do I hear! For years my world circled around you and my husband; now I have no one. I am so lonely every day, every night, and now you're gone too! How could an all-loving Father treat his child like this? Many times this past year, I have contemplated suicide. I went from 165 pounds to 103 in two months. I wasn't afraid of "Hell." I didn't want to be with a Parent who can abandon their child "Just because!" So either you want me or you don't! Just let me know. I can't live like this!

An Angry Prayer from Somebody
Waiting for a New Creation

Dear God,

How DARE you leave me here on my own?

How dare you make me have a life and then abandon me? I didn't ask to be here, and I don't want to live in this madness. It disgusts me and appalls me, and it feels even worse to find out that I turn out to BE one of those miserable human animals that are killing this planet. I am part of the problem!

ME! Who hates it all and can't wait not to be here!

I believed you when you said you would wipe every tear from our eyes.

I believed you when you said that there would be no more Death, no more pain and suffering. Me?!! Who isn't even a Christian!!! Won't go to church and don't even believe in the Bible! But I had the faith of a child, faith in Miracles, faith in Love, faith in Goodness! Well, that was a waste of bloody time, wasn't it?

A whole lifetime of believing in something that not only never transpires but appears to daily get further and further away from us!

I am sick and tired of it, I am telling you now, and I refuse to live in it any longer.

You make it happen, here and now, a new world, a new way—that's what I can pray for and that's what I want, and I won't settle for anything less.

You show me how to change the Energetic Matrix and make it work for Love, or I will sit down and cross my arms, and . . .

I WILL NOT PLAY ANYMORE!!!!!!

An Angry Prayer from a Man Who Feels Like God Has Taken Him Only Halfway

God, I am not ungrateful.

I know that I have been truly and wonderfully blessed with a smart, friendly, loving, and beautiful wife and two miraculous daughters.

I live in a great neighborhood in a small and cozy house.

I was raised by two very loving and doting parents who did their best with me and my siblings—and still do.

I grew up in a safe, secure town and received a high-quality education.

My childhood friends were loyal and honest and true to the core.

I have never suffered homelessness or addiction or financial ruin—though I have been afraid of all of them.

What I am more confused about, what I am floundering around because of is the horrible lack of direction and how you seem to play a joke on me with my career.

You used to talk to me. Now I hear nothing.

I am so grateful for so much you have given me and so

confused and distressed about why you leave this huge hole in one part of my life. It affects my family greatly. My wife has to the bear the responsibility of supporting us. You have given her a good job, but I pray you let me do my share.

Give me direction, God. Give me a good job. Or give me money so I don't need to bother you anymore.

I do love you, I do thank you, I do love you (but) I am so confused by your actions, and I miss hearing from you like I used to.

The Angry Prayer of a Worried Mom

"P" and I were married for seventeen years. Together we built a beautiful home and family, worshipped you, volunteered for you, and believed in you. Now "P" is gone, enjoying his unencumbered life, while the kids and I wonder why he abandoned us. My friends and "the church" say, "God will take care of you," "Trust in God," and "Have faith." Well, I did, and my life continues to spiral downward.

Now I am stuck with our "dream home" (his dream home actually) that I can't afford and can't sell without losing money. I am going further and further into debt to try to pay the bills. There are repairs and maintenance that need to be done, but I can't do it myself and I can't afford to hire someone to do it for me. "Look at the birds of the air; they neither sow nor reap . . . and yet your heavenly Father feeds them. Are you not of more value than they?" (Matthew 6:26–27).

I think I'd rather be a bird! I certainly don't feel very valuable. You can't even bother to send a small sense of calm or a sign that things will be better eventually? If this is a test, I'm failing miserably!

Oh, Lord, my two kids are hurting so badly. I am not able to take their hurt away, and that is killing me. I've prayed for and with them for strength and happiness. They have prayed, too. We hear nothing from you!

And I am lonely. I have wonderful friends and colleagues, but at the end of the day they go home to their families and I go home and try to keep our lives afloat. I long for the companionship of another person who will share my joys and my sorrows, someone who cares about how I feel and what I think. I believe that You care; that's what I was taught, but I don't feel it. There is no relief from the anger and hurt and fear. I search for comfort in You and there is nothing—just emptiness.

I have waited for three years now, God. When will you answer me?

I can't pray—I am weary from prayer. The more I pray the more conflicted I become.

Hope has driven me insane.

I am tired, broken, and stink of humanness.

So the only hope I have left is the hope that, before I die, this lingering suspicion I have about you will be reasoned away with enlightenment (and if you're up for some discourse so I can vent all this hateful rage, shame, guilt, and fear . . . that would be good, too).

An Angry Prayer from Someone Struggling with Belief

Oh God, every day I sense Your icy gaze.
I feel Your endless watch—staring down.
I hear Your grumbles and pious sighs.

112

Hear me, my life is NOT Yours to appraise!
My heart rejects Your furious frown!
My soul ignores Your spiteful eyes!

But NAY, You are my Lord No More!
Begone with Your psalms and petty prayer!
Begone with Your madness! BEGONE! Amen.

An Angry Prayer from a Frustrated Wife

In the Name of the Father and of the Son and of the Holy Spirit. Amen.

Dear God and my Heavenly Angels and Saints:

Please forgive my nasty, angry prayer. You know that my husband is good to me in bed and I am attracted to him, but I am also fantasizing. Please forgive me, God, for being so personal, but you know what's going on, and sometimes I forget to talk and pray to you about it. Sometimes I find it hard to pray because I am so in debt and ashamed. Lazy too. It's no wonder things aren't moving so smoothly. It seems I am always asking you for help with my own issues, and I know there are a lot of people dying and a lot of people don't have shelter, clothing, or food or loved ones.

I always thank you for the safety you have given my children and for all the children I have cared for and for the love that I have received from them, but now it is my time, God, and I don't know where to begin. I have rooted our children onto their paths of

113

*the Catholic Faith. God, I am proud of how much
they hold you in their hearts.*

*But as the third and youngest child is making her
confirmation I am so worried about my life. The
husband of twenty-five years doesn't think day care
for twenty-one years is a job, and always complains
when I ask him to do a household project or to
follow through with the yard work. Forgive me
when I want to run away after I have finished his
chores so many times. I sometimes want to give up
on my marriage or think about burning the house
down so that I don't have to clean out all the storage
crap, and then no one would see the work that my
husband has left undone, but then I remember the
vows I have made in your house, and I don't want to
put a firefighter in danger either.*

*Please, God, help me to get in shape, and help me
to love myself more, and help me to not dwell in the
past of anger and darkness. Give me strength and
please give me some signs in my daily life and in my
dreams for my life path. I love you so very much.*

*In the Name of the Father and of the Son and of
the Holy Spirit. Amen.*

An Angry Prayer from a Lost Soul

God, there is no poetry to my prayer. Poetry, like so
much else, disappeared for me a long time ago. I have
been either forgotten or deliberately forsaken by you,
God, if you even exist.

I spent the first half of my life searching for you,

O Lord, searching everywhere with endless study. Still, I am empty and without hope, angry, and finally numb, faithless, and forsaken.

Springsteen says, "In the end what we don't surrender, well, the world just strips away." God, I can only beg, plead, cry to you for so long. I have nothing left to strip away. So now I only search for anybody who God knows in order to ask God on my behalf, "Why?"

What is so wrong with me?

Whatever I may have done, I am sorry. If you tell me what I have done, O Lord, to be so cut off from you, I promise, God, to try to fix it; make it better, be better.

I will do whatever it takes if you will end the torture I have experienced since I was a child and saw a black shadow hovering behind me at all times. Even as a child I knew it was part of me, that part of me that keeps me from God.

As I have gotten older, I only feel the black shadow trailing me with my psychic eyes, but it's always nearby. Of course, I suffer from depression, and the shadow man is moving closer and closer in on me. Doctors tell me that my stress comes from some past traumatic shock, but what can I have done at so young an age to bring this upon myself?

Who could be so horrible as to be utterly forsaken by a God who is supposed to be merciful?

Why would God inflict this upon me and leave me so alone to spend every day wishing for death or waking every morning of my entire life to face yet another miserable day?

And if God is the Creator, then am I not God's creation too? Why don't I deserve parental love or bonding?

What sin could I have committed as a child to be punished with a life of poverty and loneliness and one traumatic event after another for fifty-two years?

Foreclosure, homelessness, hunger, sadness, grief: I have lived a cursed life of one loss after another. In fifty-two years I have never had more than three days when I have been content to be alive.

I carry the weariness of an eternity.

So please, God, hear my prayer: All I ask is that you just tell me why and when will this hell finally be over?

I go to church, but not to services. I go just to be alone just in case the day would ever come when something would be revealed to me.

I go to church to give private thanks when I am grateful for something, to beg when I am in more dire straits, to rest when I am weary.

So, God, while I am now mostly just numb, you can restore my soul by finally answering . . .

Why?

And when will it finally be over?

An Angry Prayer for Rose and Jakie

Dear God:

I talk at you a lot, mostly pleading, "Don't hurt me, don't let me lose any more, please don't let me get any sicker, please let me belong, please let me feel loved, please don't take my loved ones away." First my daughter (I felt so alone in that courtroom), then my mom, then my dad (he was so scared to die), and that whole business with my sister.

Of course I was sick too then. Oh, God, not my dog, Jakie—he didn't want to die that day—he fought for his life and savored it but was always afraid like me that someone would come and take it all away. I am sick, God—you know that with Lupus and not the worst but certainly the painful and limiting kind—I cannot walk well as my legs hurt, the surgery was helpful but my back is degenerating and it hurts. I want this illness to stop taking away my femininity—the walker; the Bell's palsy left its marks. My right eye isn't right, it's dry and blinks too much and doesn't close the way it used to. God, when I was a little girl at Catholic school, couldn't you cut me a break? Allowing that priest to try to touch me? Too much.

Maybe all that happened because I was too stupid or useless. God, why did you give me to my mother if she would tell me hundreds of times how I ruined her life? Couldn't you have kept me in heaven and just given me a small corner there with Jakie's spirit? God, I need help for my son as I have not been the best mother, and now we take care of each other. It is all confused, and he gets so angry at me, and I am mean to him a lot. I want someone to love me—to hold me and tell me the worst is over.

Please, God, send me some love, and if you could dial back the suffering stuff a little. Well, please keep the wonders coming. I do love You and long to see Jakie again.

Your child,
Rose

117

An Angry Prayer of Despair

Oh God of Abraham, your prophet gave birth to three separate parts recognized as religions—Judaism, Christianity, and Islam.

All three have frequently been hijacked over fifty centuries, subverting your teachings to acquire wealth and power.

Why do the elite of the religions of Abraham seemingly revel in criticizing and creating conflict with each other, often killing or maiming the innocent faithful of all three?

Why do those who claim worship and adherence to your laws find it so easy to obfuscate truth and enslave your children?

How many suffer fear rather than love, aware of the secular power wielded by these scoundrels who routinely damn secular power?

Why are we forbidden from discussing these issues in your cleansing sunlight? Are we not obliged to seek truth rather than being slaves to subversion and propaganda? Must we continue to battle ubiquitous apologists?

How many of your faithful have lost faith by perceiving these realities, then abandoning your teachings? Is this not the mystery of mysteries, the irony of ironies, the enigma of enigmas?

We sincerely need your help.

An Angry Prayer of Hope

*To hope against hope
that one voice might find another*

with companionship, in dark realms
where voice must be the only guide
to what escape might be found
amidst confusions of anger.

Must I meanwhile suffer in silence,
and blindly obey the blindly obedient?

Must I act out, and become who
would oppress me?

Are these times so different from
those before? I cannot see what
came before my eyes were first opened,
and have only what the venerable
witness of history would show me,
which teaches much, but proves little.

My anger aroused so many mornings,
subdued by drink in the evening,
is my constant reminder that
something isn't right.

O God, deliver me from anger,
from those who would fight
fire with burning fire, rather
than with cooling water.

God knows the Flood, but also
keeps the gentle Tide. There
is reason in this beyond what
we can rightly claim to know.

I pray to You, God, be with me
and all your children, and stay,
that with our imperfect vision we
might see enough to give praise
where praise is due.

An Angry Prayer from the Trusting but Exhausted

I was loved as a child but grew up in a bar without a father. . . .

I trusted God to help me.

I had asthma and struggled to breathe until my little lungs were sore. . . .

I trusted God to help me.

I ran away from God and partied up a storm as a teen. . . .

I must have trusted God through this because I didn't die.

I got married, had four children and felt abandoned and alone, yet I kept up the faith and struggled so hard, worked so hard and still . . .

I trusted God to help me.

I had back surgery, made huge mistakes, walked with God and asked him to carry me at times, trusting he would do this for us.

I went to church, read the Bible, and searched and searched for answers. After I got my BA as a full-time working single mom trying to prove to my kids there is hope to researching quantum physics, metaphysics, religion, the Bible and kept looking for help from God, success seemed to elude me but I continued to trust God to help me.

I begged and still do for forgiveness of my sins while I watch crooks steal the American dream and watch prophetic mumblings from paranoid people and conspiracy theorists come true and still try to trust God to help me.

I am thinking about moving to a cold climate where my fiancé has more family and I am hoping my lungs can take the cold because I can't afford California anymore, and, again, I am trusting God to help me.

I have been an avid reader of positive-thinking books, I have even written a book on hope, yet I have to try to remember each day what to be thankful for in the face of adversity. I keep asking and trusting God to help me.

A Prayer from Someone Who Feels Alone

O Lord, thou art One . . . does that include me as well?

I know the depths of Adam's damnation. You allowed him—and through him us, to separate.

Why?

I can look out at creation and imagine everything in it intimately connected and woven into one universal and perfect tapestry where everything from Quasar to Quark fits and is perfectly complete . . .

. . . except for me.

And, even I know, that is absurd or mad—or both.

What is this insane illusion that I call "me"? Why do I need it?

Why?

It only brings me pain, fear, and anxiety.

It's an impediment.

I know this because when "I'm" not around, talking, or scheming, or worrying; when I finally shut up to take a breath—it is then that inexplicable and causeless joy bubbles up fountain-like from some secret somewhere.

I know that fountain is You. I know it like I know my mother's kiss on my forehead.

Yet no longer than the instant it takes for me to utter, "Oh my God, what joy!" it evaporates and the fear and worry roll back in like a stone covering a tomb.

Why?

What the Hell is that all about?

I know my redeemer liveth. Yet you allow me to bang around for years—for decades really—miserable and alone.

Why? I can do nothing—I have tried everything.

I can't even get angry at you anymore.

Take "me" out, O Lord. Show me my place in that fountain and in that tapestry. Separate no longer.

An Angry Prayer of a Nonbeliever

What the hell is this? If you are there, Lord, why don't you answer? If you have answered, why can't I hear it?

I have been on this earth for over fifty-nine years. Yes, there have been times of joy, but overall my life has mainly been one of frustration and regret. It seems that every effort I have made toward love or financial solvency has ultimately ended in failure.

I have tried religion over and over. I have read the Bible, I have got down on my knees and prayed for forgiveness and salvation, and I have asked Jesus to come into my heart. I have yet to feel any comfort from that. I have tried more than a few churches, and in each one I attended I felt out of place.

It is not really you, God, I am mad at. You may well be there, I don't know, but I have pretty much come to the conclusion that no religion on earth has the answers. When I think about the concept of the Bible as "God's word," I cringe. Would a perfect God use such an imperfect medium as the written word? Why would you not put your message in our hearts or in the air we breathe if you really wanted us to hear it?

I don't know the answers, and perhaps I never will, but if you are really there I wish you would at least point me in the right direction.

An Angry Prayer from a Loving Aunt

Lord, my niece is having a hard time, and it looks like she's headed for harder times. She is angry at You that she has lost her father, and I understand how she feels. To be honest, I share some of how she feels; I don't understand how so many truly awful parents seem to live forever and inflict their cruelty on their children unendingly, and someone like my brother who loved his daughter dearly dies accidentally. I know you don't run around killing people; I don't believe it was your will for his death to happen. I know lots of kids lose one or both parents for no good reason. I just have a hard time accepting that crappy parents abound while my niece is foundering.

Please, Lord, tell me what to tell her that will help her. Amen.

A Selection of Angry Prayers from Everyday Folks

An Angry Prayer to Forgive

I've forgiven my parents and relatives.
I've forgiven my friends and enemies.
I've even forgiven myself.
You're the only one left.
So I forgive you, God.
And now I am free.

An Angry Prayer for Nothing

I asked for strength; I became painfully aware of my
*   weakness.*
I asked to be tough; I got a beating.
I asked for patience; I see how intolerant and greedy I've
*   become.*
I asked for wisdom; I became aware of my vanity and
*   folly.*
I asked for money; my lack is constant.
I asked for understanding; I'm ignorant.
I asked for love; constantly, I'm reminded of my
*   selfishness.*
I asked to be kind; I can still be brutish, and cruel, in
*   thought and deed.*
I asked for unity with another; I'm lonely.

I want you to send me nothing, make me nothing, give me
*   nothing. I want nothing from you.*
Whatever nothing is, give it to me now.
I have no idea what I need, and you are not Santa Claus.
Amen.

Prayer of an Angry Daughter and Sister

Lord, how long must I endure the lying and deliberate efforts to destroy my children and myself? How do I forgive?

I have said to You and others, "You can attempt to destroy me, but DON'T mess with my children." Forgiveness is much easier when my children are not being persecuted.

Why would you send me into a family that has no love for me or my children? Why would you place me with a mother that "devours her young"?

Why does my earthly mother feel the Puritans were justified in accusing persons of witchcraft and burning them at the stake?

My earthly mother says that she destroyed my relationships to maintain her control. Where is Love in this? Why does she believe that she will be sitting beside You on the throne on judgment day passing sentences on sinners? Why, oh God, does she feel she has to practice now to pass judgment? When I speak Your word to her— "judge not lest you be judged"—she simply says that doesn't apply to her.

Please understand my need to separate myself from my earthly family. Loose their tongues to the Truth. Let their lips burn with your purifying fire. Show my birth family the truth. I plead with You to help them see the destruction they have caused.

Have them make restitution to my children. The wounds are deep, Lord, and they are slow to heal because there is always someone who reopens the wounds.

You, God, are fully capable of restoring the years the locusts have eaten.

Please heal my children and their children. Please heal me and enable my children and myself to live victoriously. Please forgive my inability to forgive. My heart yearns to end the bitterness.

I praise you, God, for you are Most Holy.

APPENDIX OF PSALMS

*Have you ever considered the relationship between pow-*erful lyrics and music? When the sun is shining and a light breeze is blowing, there are just certain songs that need to be played with the top down on a convertible. At the office, a business atmosphere calls for a different set of tunes, probably less noticeable, maybe without any words at all. In the evening, when friends gather for a so-cial dinner, perhaps some classical music or some light, melodic jazz would establish the right atmosphere.

But when one has been abandoned by a lover, fired from work, or is feeling stepped on by the universe, it is likely that neither a sunshine/driving song, some office Muzak©, or dinner party background sound will fit this angry, resentful, lonely, or defiant situation. It's ironic that a happy song might only make a sad mood worse while the right sad song might help somebody feel less alone in their misery.

A couple years ago Jaron Lowenstein, a funny, tal-ented singer/songwriter, wrote a great breakup song called "I Pray for You" that illustrates the point well:

I haven't been to church since I don't remember when
Things were going great 'til they fell apart again
So I listened to the preacher as he told me what to do
He said you can't go hating others who have done wrong
    to you.
Sometimes we get angry, but we must not condemn.
Let the good Lord do His job and you just pray for them.

I pray your brakes go out running down a hill
I pray a flowerpot falls from a window sill and knocks
    you in the head like I'd like to
I pray your birthday comes and nobody calls
I pray you're flying high when your engine stalls
I pray all your dreams never come true
Just know wherever you are, honey, I pray for you

Indeed, when tragedy strikes, misery loves musical company, and the effect can often be very therapeutic. For whatever reason, if you have been wronged somehow, hearing a song from somebody else who is similarly suffering can speak right to your soul (perhaps one of the few times that two wrongs do make a right).

Timeless lyrics that have transcended the need for any music is the backstory for the Book of Psalms. The word *psalms* is a variation of the Greek verb "psalloo," meaning "to play an instrument," or "psalmos" for "song." The psalms are the common heart of both the Hebrew and Christian Bibles. This is pretty amazing when you consider Psalms is largely a book of lyrics whose tunes nobody knows anymore. In some ways, Psalms is like an album cover's lyric sheet without the CD inside.

In Judaism and Christianity, Psalms is both a well-used hymnal and a prayer book. Most abridged Christian Bibles consist of the New Testament and the Book of Psalms. Give or take one or two, there are 150 psalms in every Bible. Some of these 150 songs were intended as hymns for worship; others may have been just poems with no musical accompaniment intended, that is, the psalms that praise Judaic law. Most psalms have minimal or no vocal or instrumental instruction.

As many as eighty of the psalms may been written by King David, the legendary biblical figure (some say he wrote all of them). Either way, we might think of David as the Paul McCartney of Psalms. More likely, perhaps, most of those have just been ascribed to him or written in a Davidic style. Solomon, Asaph, Ethan, and the Sons of Korah are also listed as psalmists. Moses may have contributed, but that seems particularly doubtful according to many biblical researchers.

What we do know for sure is that it seems that of the 150 psalms that have come down to us, many literary patterns and forms emerge. For example, the psalms can be broken up in dozens of ways, such as by historical period, subject matter, theological theme, style, titles, and so forth.

Perhaps the most interesting door into the mystery and majesty of Psalms requires even more of the reader, the door simply labeled "Why?" Why was this particular psalm written? What emotion does it capture or evoke in the reader/hearer? Is its meaning obvious? Is there a subtext? Of all the songs of that era, why has this particular psalm been included in these 150 that have been sung, read, repeated, quoted, and contemplated for thousands of years?

Trying to understand the "why" of the psalms has led scholars to attempt to categorize the various psalms according to their perceived intent. This is done through a process called "literary criticism." Bible enthusiasts search the psalms for repeated words, phrases, and themes in order to establish some of the motifs of the passages and then group them together accordingly. So complex are many of the psalms in their theology, however, that any easy, simple categorization eventually runs into trouble. For example, as we discussed earlier, many of the psalms could fit into more than one category or have parts that fit in one category and not another.

This is the case of the lament psalms. *Lament psalm* is too weak a descriptor to apply consistently and evenly to every song of its genre, in my opinion (and sometimes *curse psalm* seems too harsh). While many of the psalms in this group do wail or grieve for one or many things, some of the lament psalms have a curse psalm flavor to them even if the psalm lacks a specific demand from God to bring pain to an enemy. The tone of many of these psalms is "God, it makes me angry that you're angry at the wrong people."

So, again, while scholars may quibble about which psalm fits best in which category, the following psalms represent the Bible's "Prayers for the Pissed Off," printed here in their original form without modification.

Psalm 5
TRUST IN GOD FOR DELIVERANCE FROM ENEMIES

To the leader: for the flutes. A Psalm of David.

Give ear to my words, O Lord;
give heed to my sighing.

Listen to the sound of my cry,
my King and my God,
for to you I pray.
O Lord, in the morning you hear my voice;
in the morning I plead my case to you, and watch.

For you are not a God who delights in wickedness;
evil will not sojourn with you.
The boastful will not stand before your eyes;
you hate all evildoers.
You destroy those who speak lies;
the Lord abhors the bloodthirsty and deceitful.

But I, through the abundance of your steadfast love,
will enter your house,
I will bow down toward your holy temple
in awe of you.
Lead me, O Lord, in your righteousness
because of my enemies;
make your way straight before me.

For there is no truth in their mouths;
their hearts are destruction;
their throats are open graves;
they flatter with their tongues.
Make them bear their guilt, O God;
let them fall by their own counsels;
because of their many transgressions cast them out,
for they have rebelled against you.

But let all who take refuge in you rejoice;
let them ever sing for joy.

Spread your protection over them,
so that those who love your name may exult in you.
For you bless the righteous, O Lord;
you cover them with favor as with a shield.

Psalm 6
PRAYER FOR RECOVERY FROM GRAVE ILLNESS

To the leader: with stringed instruments; according to
The Sheminith. A Psalm of David.

O Lord, do not rebuke me in your anger,
or discipline me in your wrath.
Be gracious to me, O Lord, for I am languishing;
O Lord, heal me, for my bones are shaking with terror.
My soul also is struck with terror,
while you, O Lord—how long?

Turn, O Lord, save my life;
deliver me for the sake of your steadfast love.
For in death there is no remembrance of you;
in Sheol who can give you praise?

I am weary with my moaning;
every night I flood my bed with tears;
I drench my couch with my weeping.
My eyes waste away because of grief;
they grow weak because of all my foes.

Depart from me, all you workers of evil,
for the Lord has heard the sound of my weeping.
The Lord has heard my supplication;
the Lord accepts my prayer.

All my enemies shall be ashamed and struck with terror;
they shall turn back, and in a moment be put to shame.

Psalm 11
SONG OF TRUST IN GOD

To the leader. Of David.

In the Lord I take refuge; how can you say to me,
"Flee like a bird to the mountains;
for look, the wicked bend the bow,
they have fitted their arrow to the string,
to shoot in the dark at the upright in heart.
If the foundations are destroyed,
what can the righteous do?"

The Lord is in his holy temple;
the Lord's throne is in heaven.
His eyes behold, his gaze examines humankind.
The Lord tests the righteous and the wicked,
and his soul hates the lover of violence.
On the wicked he will rain coals of fire and sulphur;
a scorching wind shall be the portion of their cup.
For the Lord is righteous;
he loves righteous deeds;
the upright shall behold his face.

Psalm 12
Plea for Help in Evil Times

To the leader: according to The Sheminith.
A Psalm of David.

Help, O Lord, for there is no longer anyone who is godly;
the faithful have disappeared from humankind.
They utter lies to each other;
with flattering lips and a double heart they speak.

May the Lord cut off all flattering lips,
the tongue that makes great boasts,
those who say, "With our tongues we will prevail;
our lips are our own—who is our master?"

"Because the poor are despoiled, because the needy
        groan,
I will now rise up," says the Lord;
"I will place them in the safety for which they long."
The promises of the Lord are promises that are pure,
silver refined in a furnace on the ground,
purified seven times.

You, O Lord, will protect us;
you will guard us from this generation forever.
On every side the wicked prowl,
as vileness is exalted among humankind.

Psalm 22

PLEA FOR DELIVERANCE FROM SUFFERING AND HOSTILITY

To the leader: according to The Deer of the Dawn. A Psalm of David.

My God, my God, why have you forsaken me?
Why are you so far from helping me, from the words of
    my groaning?
O my God, I cry by day, but you do not answer;
and by night, but find no rest.

Yet you are holy,
enthroned on the praises of Israel.
In you our ancestors trusted;
they trusted, and you delivered them.
To you they cried, and were saved;
in you they trusted, and were not put to shame.

But I am a worm, and not human;
scorned by others, and despised by the people.
All who see me mock at me;
they make mouths at me, they shake their heads;
"Commit your cause to the Lord; let him deliver—
let him rescue the one in whom he delights!"

Yet it was you who took me from the womb;
you kept me safe on my mother's breast.
On you I was cast from my birth,
and since my mother bore me you have been my God.
Do not be far from me,

for trouble is near
and there is no one to help.

Many bulls encircle me,
strong bulls of Bashan surround me;
they open wide their mouths at me,
like a ravening and roaring lion.

I am poured out like water,
and all my bones are out of joint;
my heart is like wax;
it is melted within my breast;
my mouth is dried up like a potsherd,
and my tongue sticks to my jaws;
you lay me in the dust of death.

For dogs are all around me;
a company of evildoers encircles me.
My hands and feet have shrivelled;
I can count all my bones.
They stare and gloat over me;
they divide my clothes among themselves,
and for my clothing they cast lots.

But you, O Lord, do not be far away!
O my help, come quickly to my aid!
Deliver my soul from the sword,
my life from the power of the dog!
Save me from the mouth of the lion!

From the horns of the wild oxen you have rescued me.
I will tell of your name to my brothers and sisters;
in the midst of the congregation I will praise you:

You who fear the Lord, praise him!
All you offspring of Jacob, glorify him;
stand in awe of him, all you offspring of Israel!
For he did not despise or abhor
the affliction of the afflicted;
he did not hide his face from me,
but heard when I cried to him.

From you comes my praise in the great congregation;
my vows I will pay before those who fear him.
The poor shall eat and be satisfied;
those who seek him shall praise the Lord.
May your hearts live forever!

All the ends of the earth shall remember
and turn to the Lord;
and all the families of the nations
shall worship before him.
For dominion belongs to the Lord,
and he rules over the nations.

To him, indeed, shall all who sleep in the earth bow
*   down;*
before him shall bow all who go down to the dust,
and I shall live for him.
Posterity will serve him;
future generations will be told about the Lord,
and proclaim his deliverance to a people yet unborn,
saying that he has done it.

Psalm 35

Prayer for Deliverance from Enemies

Of David.

> *Contend, O Lord, with those who contend with me;*
> *fight against those who fight against me!*
> *Take hold of shield and buckler,*
> *and rise up to help me!*
> *Draw the spear and javelin*
> *against my pursuers;*
> *say to my soul,*
> *"I am your salvation."*
>
> *Let them be put to shame and dishonor*
> *who seek after my life.*
> *Let them be turned back and confounded*
> *who devise evil against me.*
> *Let them be like chaff before the wind,*
> *with the angel of the Lord driving them on.*
> *Let their way be dark and slippery,*
> *with the angel of the Lord pursuing them.*
>
> *For without cause they hid their net for me;*
> *without cause they dug a pit for my life.*
> *Let ruin come on them unawares.*
> *And let the net that they hid ensnare them;*
> *let them fall in it—to their ruin.*
>
> *Then my soul shall rejoice in the Lord,*
> *exulting in his deliverance.*
> *All my bones shall say,*
> *"O Lord, who is like you?*

You deliver the weak
from those too strong for them,
the weak and needy from those who despoil them."

Malicious witnesses rise up;
they ask me about things I do not know.
They repay me evil for good;
my soul is forlorn.
But as for me, when they were sick,
I wore sackcloth;
I afflicted myself with fasting.
I prayed with head bowed on my bosom,
as though I grieved for a friend or a brother;
I went about as one who laments for a mother,
bowed down and in mourning.

But at my stumbling they gathered in glee,
they gathered together against me;
ruffians whom I did not know
tore at me without ceasing;
they impiously mocked more and more,
gnashing at me with their teeth.

How long, O Lord, will you look on?
Rescue me from their ravages,
my life from the lions!
Then I will thank you in the great congregation;
in the mighty throng I will praise you.

Do not let my treacherous enemies rejoice over me,
or those who hate me without cause wink the eye.
For they do not speak peace,
but they conceive deceitful words

against those who are quiet in the land.
They open wide their mouths against me;
they say, "Aha, Aha,
our eyes have seen it."

You have seen, O Lord; do not be silent!
O Lord, do not be far from me!
Wake up! Bestir yourself for my defense,
for my cause, my God and my Lord!
Vindicate me, O Lord, my God,
according to your righteousness,
and do not let them rejoice over me.
Do not let them say to themselves,
"Aha, we have our heart's desire."
Do not let them say, "We have swallowed you up."

Let all those who rejoice at my calamity
be put to shame and confusion;
let those who exalt themselves against me
be clothed with shame and dishonor.

Let those who desire my vindication
shout for joy and be glad,
and say evermore,
"Great is the Lord,
who delights in the welfare of his servant."
Then my tongue shall tell of your righteousness
and of your praise all day long.

Psalm 37

EXHORTATION TO PATIENCE AND TRUST

Of David.

Do not fret because of the wicked;
do not be envious of wrongdoers,
for they will soon fade like the grass,
and wither like the green herb.

Trust in the Lord, and do good;
so you will live in the land, and enjoy security.
Take delight in the Lord,
and he will give you the desires of your heart.

Commit your way to the Lord;
trust in him, and he will act.
He will make your vindication shine like the light,
and the justice of your cause like the noonday.

Be still before the Lord, and wait patiently for him;
do not fret over those who prosper in their way,
over those who carry out evil devices.

Refrain from anger, and forsake wrath.
Do not fret—it leads only to evil.
For the wicked shall be cut off,
but those who wait for the Lord shall inherit the land.

Yet a little while, and the wicked will be no more;
though you look diligently for their place, they will not be
*   there.*
But the meek shall inherit the land,
and delight themselves in abundant prosperity.

The wicked plot against the righteous,
and gnash their teeth at them;
but the Lord laughs at the wicked,
for he sees that their day is coming.

The wicked draw the sword and bend their bows
to bring down the poor and needy,
to kill those who walk uprightly;
their sword shall enter their own heart,
and their bows shall be broken.

Better is a little that the righteous person has
than the abundance of many wicked.
For the arms of the wicked shall be broken,
but the Lord upholds the righteous.

The Lord knows the days of the blameless,
and their heritage will abide forever;
they are not put to shame in evil times,
in the days of famine they have abundance.

But the wicked perish,
and the enemies of the Lord are like the glory of the
pastures;
they vanish—like smoke they vanish away.

The wicked borrow, and do not pay back,
but the righteous are generous and keep giving;
for those blessed by the Lord shall inherit the land,
but those cursed by him shall be cut off.

Our steps are made firm by the Lord,
when he delights in our way;

though we stumble, we shall not fall headlong,
for the Lord holds us by the hand.

I have been young, and now am old,
yet I have not seen the righteous forsaken
or their children begging bread.
They are ever giving liberally and lending,
and their children become a blessing.

Depart from evil, and do good;
so you shall abide forever.
For the Lord loves justice;
he will not forsake his faithful ones.

The righteous shall be kept safe forever,
but the children of the wicked shall be cut off.
The righteous shall inherit the land,
and live in it forever.

The mouths of the righteous utter wisdom,
and their tongues speak justice.
The law of their God is in their hearts;
their steps do not slip.

The wicked watch for the righteous,
and seek to kill them.
The Lord will not abandon them to their power,
or let them be condemned when they are brought to trial.

Wait for the Lord, and keep to his way,
and he will exalt you to inherit the land;
you will look on the destruction of the wicked.

I have seen the wicked oppressing,
and towering like a cedar of Lebanon.
Again I passed by, and they were no more;
though I sought them, they could not be found.

Mark the blameless, and behold the upright,
for there is posterity for the peaceable.
But transgressors shall be altogether destroyed;
the posterity of the wicked shall be cut off.

The salvation of the righteous is from the Lord;
he is their refuge in the time of trouble.
The Lord helps them and rescues them;
he rescues them from the wicked, and saves them,
because they take refuge in him.

Psalm 40
THANKSGIVING FOR DELIVERANCE AND PRAYER FOR HELP

To the leader. Of David. A Psalm.

I waited patiently for the Lord;
he inclined to me and heard my cry.
He drew me up from the desolate pit,
out of the miry bog,
and set my feet upon a rock,
making my steps secure.
He put a new song in my mouth,
a song of praise to our God.
Many will see and fear,
and put their trust in the Lord.

Happy are those who make
the Lord their trust,
who do not turn to the proud,
to those who go astray after false gods.
You have multiplied, O Lord my God,
your wondrous deeds and your thoughts toward us;
none can compare with you.
Were I to proclaim and tell of them,
they would be more than can be counted.

Sacrifice and offering you do not desire,
but you have given me an open ear.
Burnt offering and sin offering
you have not required.
Then I said, "Here I am;
in the scroll of the book it is written of me.
I delight to do your will, O my God;
your law is within my heart."

I have told the glad news of deliverance
in the great congregation;
see, I have not restrained my lips,
as you know, O Lord.
I have not hidden your saving help within my heart,
I have spoken of your faithfulness and your salvation;
I have not concealed your steadfast love and your
    faithfulness
from the great congregation.

Do not, O Lord, withhold
your mercy from me;
let your steadfast love and your faithfulness
keep me safe forever.

For evils have encompassed me
without number;
my iniquities have overtaken me,
until I cannot see;
they are more than the hairs of my head,
and my heart fails me.

Be pleased, O Lord, to deliver me;
O Lord, make haste to help me.
Let all those be put to shame and confusion
who seek to snatch away my life;
let those be turned back and brought to dishonor
who desire my hurt.
Let those be appalled because of their shame
who say to me, "Aha, Aha!"

But may all who seek you
rejoice and be glad in you;
may those who love your salvation
say continually, "Great is the Lord!"
As for me, I am poor and needy,
but the Lord takes thought for me.
You are my help and my deliverer;
do not delay, O my God.

Psalm 44

NATIONAL LAMENT AND PRAYER

To the leader. Of the Korahites. A Maskil.

We have heard with our ears, O God,
our ancestors have told us,

what deeds you performed in their days,
in the days of old:
you with your own hand drove out the nations,
but them you planted;
you afflicted the peoples,
but them you set free;
for not by their own sword did they win the land,
nor did their own arm give them victory;
but your right hand, and your arm,
and the light of your countenance,
for you delighted in them.

You are my King and my God;
you command victories for Jacob.
Through you we push down our foes;
through your name we tread down our assailants.
For not in my bow do I trust,
nor can my sword save me.
But you have saved us from our foes,
and have put to confusion those who hate us.
In God we have boasted continually,
and we will give thanks to your name forever. Selah

Yet you have rejected us and abased us,
and have not gone out with our armies.
You made us turn back from the foe,
and our enemies have taken spoil.
You have made us like sheep for slaughter,
and have scattered us among the nations.
You have sold your people for a trifle,
demanding no high price for them.

You have made us the taunt of our neighbors,
the derision and scorn of those around us.

You have made us a byword among the nations,
a laughingstock among the peoples.
All day long my disgrace is before me,
and shame has covered my face
at the words of the taunters and revilers,
at the sight of the enemy and the avenger.

All this has come upon us,
yet we have not forgotten you,
or been false to your covenant.
Our heart has not turned back,
nor have our steps departed from your way,
yet you have broken us in the haunt of jackals,
and covered us with deep darkness.

If we had forgotten the name of our God,
or spread out our hands to a strange god,
would not God discover this?
For he knows the secrets of the heart.
Because of you we are being killed all day long,
and accounted as sheep for the slaughter.

Rouse yourself! Why do you sleep, O Lord?
Awake, do not cast us off forever!
Why do you hide your face?
Why do you forget our affliction and oppression?
For we sink down to the dust;
our bodies cling to the ground.
Rise up, come to our help.
Redeem us for the sake of your steadfast love.

Psalm 52

JUDGMENT ON THE DECEITFUL

To the leader. A Maskil of David, when Doeg the Edomite came to Saul and said to him, "David has come to the house of Ahimelech."

Why do you boast, O mighty one,
of mischief done against the godly?
All day long you are plotting destruction.
Your tongue is like a sharp razor,
you worker of treachery.
You love evil more than good,
and lying more than speaking the truth. Selah
You love all words that devour,
O deceitful tongue.

But God will break you down forever;
he will snatch and tear you from your tent;
he will uproot you from the land of the living. Selah
The righteous will see, and fear,
and will laugh at the evildoer, saying,
"See the one who would not take
refuge in God,
but trusted in abundant riches,
and sought refuge in wealth!"

But I am like a green olive tree
in the house of God.
I trust in the steadfast love of God
forever and ever.
I will thank you forever,
because of what you have done.

In the presence of the faithful
I will proclaim thy name, for it is good.

Psalm 54
PRAYER FOR VINDICATION

To the leader: with stringed instruments. A Maskil of David, when the Ziphites went and told Saul, "David is in hiding among us."

Save me, O God, by your name,
and vindicate me by your might.
Hear my prayer, O God;
give ear to the words of my mouth.

For the insolent have risen against me,
the ruthless seek my life;
they do not set God before them. Selah

But surely, God is my helper;
the Lord is the upholder of my life.
He will repay my enemies for their evil.
In your faithfulness, put an end to them.

With a freewill offering I will sacrifice to you;
I will give thanks to your name, O Lord, for it is good.
For he has delivered me from every trouble,
and my eye has looked in triumph on my enemies.

Psalm 56
TRUST IN GOD UNDER PERSECUTION

To the leader: according to The Dove on Far-off
Terebinths. Of David. A Miktam, when the Philistines
seized him in Gath.

Be gracious to me, O God, for people trample on me;
all day long foes oppress me;
my enemies trample on me all day long,
for many fight against me.
O Most High, when I am afraid,
I put my trust in you.
In God, whose word I praise,
in God I trust; I am not afraid;
what can flesh do to me?

All day long they seek to injure my cause;
all their thoughts are against me for evil.
They stir up strife, they lurk,
they watch my steps.
As they hoped to have my life,
so repay them for their crime;
in wrath cast down the peoples, O God!

You have kept count of my tossings;
put my tears in your bottle.
Are they not in your record?
Then my enemies will retreat
in the day when I call.
This I know, that God is for me.
In God, whose word I praise,
in the Lord, whose word I praise,

in God I trust; I am not afraid.
What can a mere mortal do to me?

My vows to you I must perform, O God;
I will render thank offerings to you.
For you have delivered my soul from death,
and my feet from falling,
so that I may walk before God
in the light of life.

Psalm 58
PRAYER FOR VENGEANCE

To the leader: Do Not Destroy. Of David. A Miktam.

Do you indeed decree what is right, you gods?
Do you judge people fairly?
No, in your hearts you devise wrongs;
your hands deal out violence on earth.

The wicked go astray from the womb;
they err from their birth, speaking lies.
They have venom like the venom of a serpent,
like the deaf adder that stops its ear,
so that it does not hear the voice of charmers
or of the cunning enchanter.

O God, break the teeth in their mouths;
tear out the fangs of the young lions, O Lord!
Let them vanish like water that runs away;
like grass let them be trodden down and wither.

Let them be like the snail that dissolves into slime;
like the untimely birth that never sees the sun.
Sooner than your pots can feel the heat of thorns,
whether green or ablaze, may he sweep them away!

The righteous will rejoice when they see vengeance done;
they will bathe their feet in the blood of the wicked.
People will say, "Surely there is a reward for the
*   righteous;*
surely there is a God who judges on earth."

Psalm 60
PRAYER FOR NATIONAL VICTORY AFTER DEFEAT

To the leader: according to the Lily of the Covenant. A Miktam of David; for instruction; when he struggled with Aram-naharaim and with Aram-zobah, and when Joab on his return killed twelve thousand Edomites in the Valley of Salt.

O God, you have rejected us, broken our defenses;
you have been angry; now restore us!
You have caused the land to quake; you have torn it open;
repair the cracks in it, for it is tottering.
You have made your people suffer hard things;
you have given us wine to drink that made us reel.

You have set up a banner for those who fear you,
to rally to it out of bowshot. Selah
Give victory with your right hand, and answer us,
so that those whom you love may be rescued.

God has promised in his sanctuary:
"With exultation I will divide up Shechem,
and portion out the Vale of Succoth.
Gilead is mine, and Manasseh is mine;
Ephraim is my helmet;
Judah is my scepter.
Moab is my washbasin;
on Edom I hurl my shoe;
over Philistia I shout in triumph."

Who will bring me to the fortified city?
Who will lead me to Edom?
Have you not rejected us, O God?
You do not go out, O God, with our armies.
O grant us help against the foe,
for human help is worthless.
With God we shall do valiantly;
it is he who will tread down our foes.

Psalm 69

PRAYER FOR DELIVERANCE FROM PERSECUTION

To the leader: according to Lilies. Of David.

Save me, O God,
for the waters have come up to my neck.
I sink in deep mire,
where there is no foothold;
I have come into deep waters,
and the flood sweeps over me.
I am weary with my crying;

my throat is parched.
My eyes grow dim
with waiting for my God.

More in number than the hairs of my head
are those who hate me without cause;
many are those who would destroy me,
my enemies who accuse me falsely.
What I did not steal
must I now restore?
O God, you know my folly;
the wrongs I have done are not hidden from you.

Do not let those who hope in you be put to shame
        because of me,
O Lord God of hosts;
do not let those who seek you be dishonored
        because of me,
O God of Israel.
It is for your sake that I have borne reproach,
that shame has covered my face.
I have become a stranger to my kindred,
an alien to my mother's children.

It is zeal for your house that has consumed me;
the insults of those who insult you have fallen on me.
When I humbled my soul with fasting,
they insulted me for doing so.
When I made sackcloth my clothing,
I became a byword to them.
I am the subject of gossip for those who sit in the gate,
and the drunkards make songs about me.

But as for me, my prayer is to you, O Lord.
At an acceptable time, O God,
in the abundance of your steadfast love, answer me.
With your faithful help rescue me
from sinking in the mire;
let me be delivered from my enemies
and from the deep waters.
Do not let the flood sweep over me,
or the deep swallow me up,
or the Pit close its mouth over me.

Answer me, O Lord, for your steadfast love is good;
according to your abundant mercy, turn to me.
Do not hide your face from your servant,
for I am in distress—make haste to answer me.
Draw near to me, redeem me,
set me free because of my enemies.

You know the insults I receive,
and my shame and dishonor;
my foes are all known to you.
Insults have broken my heart,
so that I am in despair.
I looked for pity, but there was none;
and for comforters, but I found none.
They gave me poison for food,
and for my thirst they gave me vinegar to drink.

Let their table be a trap for them,
a snare for their allies.
Let their eyes be darkened so that they cannot see,
and make their loins tremble continually.
Pour out your indignation upon them,

and let your burning anger overtake them.
May their camp be a desolation;
let no one live in their tents.
For they persecute those whom you have struck down,
and those whom you have wounded, they attack still
    more.
Add guilt to their guilt;
may they have no acquittal from you.
Let them be blotted out of the book of the living;
let them not be enrolled among the righteous.
But I am lowly and in pain;
let your salvation, O God, protect me.

I will praise the name of God with a song;
I will magnify him with thanksgiving.
This will please the Lord more than an ox
or a bull with horns and hoofs.
Let the oppressed see it and be glad;
you who seek God, let your hearts revive.
For the Lord hears the needy,
and does not despise his own that are in bonds.

Let heaven and earth praise him,
the seas and everything that moves in them.
For God will save Zion
and rebuild the cities of Judah;
and his servants shall live there and possess it;
the children of his servants shall inherit it,
and those who love his name shall live in it.

Psalm 74

PLEA FOR HELP IN TIME OF NATIONAL HUMILIATION

A Maskil of Asaph.

O God, why do you cast us off forever?
Why does your anger smoke against the sheep of your
pasture?
Remember your congregation, which you acquired long
ago,
which you redeemed to be the tribe of your heritage.
Remember Mount Zion, where you came to dwell.
Direct your steps to the perpetual ruins;
the enemy has destroyed everything in the sanctuary.

Your foes have roared within your holy place;
they set up their emblems there.
At the upper entrance they hacked
the wooden trellis with axes.
And then, with hatchets and hammers,
they smashed all its carved work.
They set your sanctuary on fire;
they desecrated the dwelling place of your name,
bringing it to the ground.
They said to themselves, "We will utterly subdue them";
they burned all the meeting places of God in the land.

We do not see our emblems;
there is no longer any prophet,
and there is no one among us who knows how long.
How long, O God, is the foe to scoff?
Is the enemy to revile your name forever?

Why do you hold back your hand;
why do you keep your hand in your bosom?

Yet God my King is from of old,
working salvation in the earth.
You divided the sea by your might;
you broke the heads of the dragons in the waters.
You crushed the heads of Leviathan;
you gave him as food for the creatures of the wilderness.
You cut openings for springs and torrents;
you dried up ever-flowing streams.
Yours is the day, yours also the night;
you established the luminaries and the sun.
You have fixed all the bounds of the earth;
you made summer and winter.

Remember this, O Lord, how the enemy scoffs,
and an impious people reviles your name.
Do not deliver the soul of your dove to the wild animals;
do not forget the life of your poor forever.

Have regard for your covenant,
for the dark places of the land are full of the haunts of
        violence.
Do not let the downtrodden be put to shame;
let the poor and needy praise your name.
Rise up, O God, plead your cause;
remember how the impious scoff at you all day long.
Do not forget the clamor of your foes,
the uproar of your adversaries that goes up continually.

Psalm 79
PLEA FOR MERCY FOR JERUSALEM

A Psalm of Asaph.

O God, the nations have come into your inheritance;
they have defiled your holy temple;
they have laid Jerusalem in ruins.
They have given the bodies of your servants
to the birds of the air for food,
the flesh of your faithful to the wild animals of the earth.
They have poured out their blood like water
all around Jerusalem,
and there was no one to bury them.
We have become a taunt to our neighbors,
mocked and derided by those around us.

How long, O Lord? Will you be angry forever?
Will your jealous wrath burn like fire?
Pour out your anger on the nations
that do not know you,
and on the kingdoms
that do not call on your name.
For they have devoured Jacob
and laid waste his habitation.

Do not remember against us the iniquities of our
ancestors;
let your compassion come speedily to meet us,
for we are brought very low.
Help us, O God of our salvation,
for the glory of your name;

deliver us, and forgive our sins,
for your name's sake.
Why should the nations say,
"Where is their God?"
Let the avenging of the outpoured blood of your servants
be known among the nations before our eyes.

Let the groans of the prisoners come before you;
according to your great power preserve those doomed
      to die.
Return sevenfold into the bosom of our neighbors
the taunts with which they taunted you, O Lord!
Then we your people, the flock of your pasture,
will give thanks to you forever;
from generation to generation we will recount your
      praise.

Psalm 80
PRAYER FOR ISRAEL'S RESTORATION

To the leader: on Lilies, a Covenant. Of Asaph. A Psalm.

Give ear, O Shepherd of Israel,
you who lead Joseph like a flock!
You who are enthroned upon the cherubim, shine forth
before Ephraim and Benjamin and Manasseh.
Stir up your might,
and come to save us!

Restore us, O God;
let your face shine, that we may be saved.

Appendix of Psalms

O Lord God of hosts,
how long will you be angry with your people's prayers?
You have fed them with the bread of tears,
and given them tears to drink in full measure.
You make us the scorn of our neighbors;
our enemies laugh among themselves.

Restore us, O God of hosts;
let your face shine, that we may be saved.

You brought a vine out of Egypt;
you drove out the nations and planted it.
You cleared the ground for it;
it took deep root and filled the land.
The mountains were covered with its shade,
the mighty cedars with its branches;
it sent out its branches to the sea,
and its shoots to the River.
Why then have you broken down its walls,
so that all who pass along the way pluck its fruit?
The boar from the forest ravages it,
and all that move in the field feed on it.

Turn again, O God of hosts;
look down from heaven, and see;
have regard for this vine,
the stock that your right hand planted.
They have burned it with fire, they have cut it down;
may they perish at the rebuke of your countenance.
But let your hand be upon the one at your right hand,
the one whom you made strong for yourself.
Then we will never turn back from you;

give us life, and we will call on your name.

Restore us, O Lord God of hosts;
let your face shine, that we may be saved.

Psalm 83
PRAYER FOR JUDGMENT ON ISRAEL'S FOES

A Song. A Psalm of Asaph.

O God, do not keep silence;
do not hold your peace or be still, O God!
Even now your enemies are in tumult;
those who hate you have raised their heads.
They lay crafty plans against your people;
they consult together against those you protect.
They say, "Come, let us wipe them out as a nation;
let the name of Israel be remembered no more."
They conspire with one accord;
against you they make a covenant—
the tents of Edom and the Ishmaelites,
Moab and the Hagrites,
Gebal and Ammon and Amalek,
Philistia with the inhabitants of Tyre;
Assyria also has joined them;
they are the strong arm of the children of Lot. Selah

Do to them as you did to Midian,
as to Sisera and Jabin at the Wadi Kishon,
who were destroyed at En-dor,
who became dung for the ground.

Make their nobles like Oreb and Zeeb,
all their princes like Zebah and Zalmunna,
who said, "Let us take the pastures of God
for our own possession."

O my God, make them like whirling dust,
like chaff before the wind.
As fire consumes the forest,
as the flame sets the mountains ablaze,
so pursue them with your tempest
and terrify them with your hurricane.
Fill their faces with shame,
so that they may seek your name, O Lord.
Let them be put to shame and dismayed forever;
let them perish in disgrace.
Let them know that you alone,
whose name is the Lord,
are the Most High over all the earth.

Psalm 94

GOD THE AVENGER OF THE RIGHTEOUS

O Lord, you God of vengeance,
you God of vengeance, shine forth!
Rise up, O judge of the earth;
give to the proud what they deserve!
O Lord, how long shall the wicked,
how long shall the wicked exult?

They pour out their arrogant words;
all the evildoers boast.
They crush your people, O Lord,

and afflict your heritage.
They kill the widow and the stranger,
they murder the orphan,
and they say, "The Lord does not see;
the God of Jacob does not perceive."

Understand, O dullest of the people;
fools, when will you be wise?
He who planted the ear, does he not hear?
He who formed the eye, does he not see?
He who disciplines the nations,
he who teaches knowledge to humankind,
does he not chastise?
The Lord knows our thoughts,
that they are but an empty breath.

Happy are those whom you discipline, O Lord,
and whom you teach out of your law,
giving them respite from days of trouble,
until a pit is dug for the wicked.
For the Lord will not forsake his people;
he will not abandon his heritage;
for justice will return to the righteous,
and all the upright in heart will follow it.

Who rises up for me against the wicked?
Who stands up for me against evildoers?
If the Lord had not been my help,
my soul would soon have lived in the land of silence.
When I thought, "My foot is slipping,"
your steadfast love, O Lord, held me up.
When the cares of my heart are many,
your consolations cheer my soul.

Can wicked rulers be allied with you,
those who contrive mischief by statute?
They band together against the life of the righteous,
and condemn the innocent to death.
But the Lord has become my stronghold,
and my God the rock of my refuge.
He will repay them for their iniquity
and wipe them out for their wickedness;
the Lord our God will wipe them out.

Psalm 109
PRAYER FOR VINDICATION AND VENGEANCE

To the leader. Of David. A Psalm.

Do not be silent, O God of my praise.
For wicked and deceitful mouths are opened against me,
speaking against me with lying tongues.
They beset me with words of hate,
and attack me without cause.
In return for my love they accuse me,
even while I make prayer for them.
So they reward me evil for good,
and hatred for my love.

They say, "Appoint a wicked man against him;
let an accuser stand on his right.
When he is tried, let him be found guilty;
let his prayer be counted as sin.
May his days be few;
may another seize his position.
May his children be orphans,

and his wife a widow.
May his children wander about and beg;
may they be driven out of the ruins they inhabit.
May the creditor seize all that he has;
may strangers plunder the fruits of his toil.
May there be no one to do him a kindness,
nor anyone to pity his orphaned children.
May his posterity be cut off;
may his name be blotted out in the second generation.
May the iniquity of his father be remembered before
    the Lord,
and do not let the sin of his mother be blotted out.
Let them be before the Lord continually,
and may his memory be cut off from the earth.
For he did not remember to show kindness,
but pursued the poor and needy
and the brokenhearted to their death.
He loved to curse; let curses come on him.
He did not like blessing; may it be far from him.
He clothed himself with cursing as his coat,
may it soak into his body like water,
like oil into his bones.
May it be like a garment that he wraps around himself,
like a belt that he wears every day."

May that be the reward of my accusers from the Lord,
of those who speak evil against my life.
But you, O Lord my Lord,
act on my behalf for your name's sake;
because your steadfast love is good, deliver me.
For I am poor and needy,
and my heart is pierced within me.
I am gone like a shadow at evening;

I am shaken off like a locust.
My knees are weak through fasting;
my body has become gaunt.
I am an object of scorn to my accusers;
when they see me, they shake their heads.

Help me, O Lord my God!
Save me according to your steadfast love.
Let them know that this is your hand;
you, O Lord, have done it.
Let them curse, but you will bless.
Let my assailants be put to shame; may your servant
    be glad.
May my accusers be clothed with dishonor;
may they be wrapped in their own shame as in a mantle.
With my mouth I will give great thanks to the Lord;
I will praise him in the midst of the throng.
For he stands at the right hand of the needy,
to save them from those who would condemn them
    to death.

Psalm 137
LAMENT OVER THE DESTRUCTION OF JERUSALEM

By the rivers of Babylon—
there we sat down and there we wept
when we remembered Zion.
On the willows there
we hung up our harps.
For there our captors
asked us for songs,

168

and our tormentors asked for mirth, saying,
"Sing us one of the songs of Zion!"

How could we sing the Lord's song
in a foreign land?
If I forget you, O Jerusalem,
let my right hand wither!
Let my tongue cling to the roof of my mouth,
if I do not remember you,
if I do not set Jerusalem
above my highest joy.

Remember, O Lord, against the Edomites
the day of Jerusalem's fall,
how they said, "Tear it down! Tear it down!
Down to its foundations!"
O daughter Babylon, you devastator!
Happy shall they be who pay you back
what you have done to us!
Happy shall they be who take your little ones
and dash them against the rock!

Psalm 139

THE INESCAPABLE GOD

To the leader. Of David. A Psalm.

O Lord, you have searched me and known me.
You know when I sit down and when I rise up;
you discern my thoughts from far away.
You search out my path and my lying down,

and are acquainted with all my ways.
Even before a word is on my tongue,
O Lord, you know it completely.
You hem me in, behind and before,
and lay your hand upon me.
Such knowledge is too wonderful for me;
it is so high that I cannot attain it.

Where can I go from your spirit?
Or where can I flee from your presence?
If I ascend to heaven, you are there;
if I make my bed in Sheol, you are there.
If I take the wings of the morning
and settle at the farthest limits of the sea,
even there your hand shall lead me,
and your right hand shall hold me fast.
If I say, "Surely the darkness shall cover me,
and the light around me become night,"
even the darkness is not dark to you;
the night is as bright as the day,
for darkness is as light to you.

For it was you who formed my inward parts;
you knit me together in my mother's womb.
I praise you, for I am fearfully and wonderfully made.
Wonderful are your works;
that I know very well.
My frame was not hidden from you,
when I was being made in secret,
intricately woven in the depths of the earth.
Your eyes beheld my unformed substance.
In your book were written
all the days that were formed for me,

when none of them as yet existed.
How weighty to me are your thoughts, O God!
How vast is the sum of them!
I try to count them—they are more than the sand;
I come to the end—I am still with you.

O that you would kill the wicked, O God,
and that the bloodthirsty would depart from me—
those who speak of you maliciously,
and lift themselves up against you for evil!
Do I not hate those who hate you, O Lord?
And do I not loathe those who rise up against you?
I hate them with perfect hatred;
I count them my enemies.
Search me, O God, and know my heart;
test me and know my thoughts.
See if there is any wicked way in me,
and lead me in the way everlasting.

Psalm 143
PRAYER FOR DELIVERANCE FROM ENEMIES

A Psalm of David.

Hear my prayer, O Lord;
give ear to my supplications in your faithfulness;
answer me in your righteousness.
Do not enter into judgment with your servant,
for no one living is righteous before you.

For the enemy has pursued me,
crushing my life to the ground,

making me sit in darkness like those long dead.
Therefore my spirit faints within me;
my heart within me is appalled.

I remember the days of old,
I think about all your deeds,
I meditate on the works of your hands.
I stretch out my hands to you;
my soul thirsts for you like a parched land. Selah

Answer me quickly, O Lord;
my spirit fails.
Do not hide your face from me,
or I shall be like those who go down to the Pit.
Let me hear of your steadfast love in the morning,
for in you I put my trust.
Teach me the way I should go,
for to you I lift up my soul.

Save me, O Lord, from my enemies;
I have fled to you for refuge.
Teach me to do your will,
for you are my God.
Let your good spirit lead me
on a level path.

For your name's sake, O Lord, preserve my life.
In your righteousness bring me out of trouble.
In your steadfast love cut off my enemies,
and destroy all my adversaries,
for I am your servant.

ACKNOWLEDGMENTS

You know all those author acknowledgments that begin, "I'd like to thank my lovely wife and brilliant editor without whom none of this would be possible"? Yeah, about that.

Turns out all those are true. I'd like to thank my lovely wife, Margery, and my brilliant editor, Gary Jansen, without whom none of this would be possible. Margery is also brilliant (and Gary is also lovely), and it's impossible to underestimate their contributions. Peter Miller, the Global Lion, would beat them both in a roaring contest, however, and I am lucky to have an agent whose heart is as big as his reputation.

I'd also like to thank my caring families and in particular my sons, Garr and Campbell, for their patience and support during a project that started when they were small and stole a weekend or two along their way to college; my dogs Dizzy and Jack, who kept me company on the porch all those late nights; and all the servers at the Blue Plate Restaurant group for the delicious food and free Wi-Fi. Yes, I would like some more iced tea, thank you.

It also helped so much to have sometimes confused but understanding bosses at Hubbard Broadcasting, Premiere Radio Networks, and my bishop, the Right Rev. Brian Prior of the Episcopal Church in Minnesota, my friend and colleague the Rev. Beth Royalty and the folks of St. Clement's Episcopal Church. Also, I owe a great deal to an idea incubator like Columbia Theological Seminary in Atlanta, where this all got started, and specifically to Dr. Christine Roy Yoder, Dr. Kathleen O'Connor, and Dr. Walter Brueggemann—I am sure that I am long forgotten as a student, but your mix of humor and intelligence instructs me to this day. Dr. Shirley Guthrie, who art in heaven, hallowed be thy name.

Every expert, every author, every pastor and public figure I interviewed for this book patiently took my many calls, sat down with me in person or on the radio, or returned my e-mails. Sorry to be such a pest, especially to Dr. Judith Orloff! Thank you all for helping me get it right.

When it comes to the identity of other people—parishioners or patients—that pass through this book, I got it wrong on purpose. Everybody's name, age, circumstance, time frame, and location are either used with express permission or obscured to protect the privacy of their health care no matter how long ago the exchange took place. It's difficult to maintain the line between *truth* and *fact,* but while the dialogue that I relate in the book is truthful, any factual detail that could possibly indicate a patient's name or condition has been fictionalized.

Finally, I want to acknowledge that the main intention of this book was to honor God by furthering the conversation about the appropriateness of angry prayer, and I would like to thank any future author for picking up my mantle should I be caught up in a whirlwind of criticism.